The
Homeschool Mom's
AWESOME IDEAS
JOURNAL

WITH PRACTICAL, PROVEN ADVICE FROM
HUNDREDS OF HOMESCHOOL FAMILIES
PLUS
YOUR OWN BRAINSTORMS,
PLANS AND DREAMS TO MAKE
YOUR HOMESCHOOL SOAR

Compiled by Jim Erskine

HOMEWAY PRESS
WWW.HOMEWAYPRESS.NET

THE HOMESCHOOL MOM'S AWESOME IDEAS JOURNAL
compiled by Jim Erskine

Published by
Homeway Press
PO Box 1187
Canmer, KY 42722

www.homeschoolfreebieoftheday.com

To all our friends who contributed their ideas, tips, and hard-earned wisdom to this journal, we thank you.

TABLE OF CONTENTS

Where this Journal came from:

Over the past ten years, we've made it a point to regularly ask readers of our homeschooling websites* all sorts of questions about both their homeschool successes ("What has been your all-time favorite homeschooling activity?") and their mistakes ("If you could start your homeschooling over again, what would you do differently, and why?"). During that time, well over two thousand homeschooling families have responded, and in their replies we've received all sorts of amazing answers, many full of wisdom, practical ideas, real-life advice and experiences. This journal is filled with great ideas and advice gleaned from that treasure trove.

Many of the best of these have been compiled in the sections of this journal. They are not organized beyond that, however, simply because we want you to take your time - with a highlighter and pen in hand - to read through EVERY ONE of these ideas and suggestions. Then filter them through your own experiences and expectations and add your own thoughts and ideas to make this journal your own. Highlight ideas that interest you. Jot down notes to yourself as you go through them (we've left plenty of room for you to use, so use it). Write down things that you want to try, or even want to avoid. Tweak suggestions to make them your own. Make lists of things that work for your family. Create a "Homeschool Bucket List" of things you want to be sure to do with your kids.

As you go through this journal, you'll find that one idea can easily spark another and another, and you will probably find many here that you can tweak and adapt to your own family situation. The ideas included here are definitely valuable to you..."real life" experiences that other homeschooling parents wanted to share, to help YOU have the best homeschool experiences possible. But your own contribution can make this journal priceless. Just start wherever you wish, and dig in. You're sure to strike gold... and in the process will create a journal that reflects your own ideas, goals, plans and dreams to make your own homeschool soar higher than it ever has before.

– Jim Erskine, editor
Homeway Press
HomewayPress.net

*FYI, Our homeschooling sites are:
HomeschoolFreebieOfTheDay.com
HomeschoolRadioShows.com
TheHomemakersMentor.com

Come visit us, please.

20 GREAT REASONS TO HOMESCHOOL

BY JIM ERSKINE

FAVORITE ACTIVITY IDEAS:

WE HAVE MADE A HUGE HISTORY TIMELINE THAT INCORPORATES WORLD HISTORY, GREEK/BYZANTINE HISTORY, RUSSIAN HISTORY AND CANADIAN HISTORY. IT HAS FOUR LINES AND WHAT WAS HAPPENING IN THESE AREAS LINES UP. WE ARE OF GREEK AND RUSSIAN BACKGROUND AND NEED THE KIDS TO BE ABLE TO SEE ALL THESE STREAMS FITTING TOGETHER. THE TIME LINE IS BIG ENOUGH THAT IT HAS ROOM FOR ALL THE CHILDREN TO ADD TO IT. ALL YOU REALLY NEED IS A LARGE BLANK WALL AND A ROLL OF PAPER. GUESTS THAT COME TO OUR HOUSE SPEND HOURS LOOKING AT OUR TIMELINE. THEY FIND IT FASCINATING TO SEE WHAT WAS GOING ON AT THE SAME TIME IN HISTORY.

MY CHILDREN HAVE ALL LOVED MAKING A HUMAN BODY TO HANG ON THE WALL. I USE A ROLL OF TEAR AWAY STABILIZER AND TRACE AROUND EACH CHILD. I HAVE COPIES OF BODY PARTS (KIDNEYS, BRAINS, LUNGS, LIVER, ETC.) THAT EACH PERSON COLORS AND CUTS OUT. WE VELCRO THE PART TO THE HUMAN SHAPE SO THEY CAN PRACTICE PUTTING THE PART IN THE RIGHT PLACE. THE CHILDREN CAN DECORATE THEIR FACE AND PERSONALIZE IT.

FIELD TRIPS, FIELD TRIPS, FIELD TRIPS. WE'VE DONE SIMPLE ONES, SUCH AS GOING TO OUR LOCAL BAKERY'S KITCHEN, TO MORE INVOLVED ONES LIKE GOING TO FOSSIL PARK IN OH (A TWO-HOUR DRIVE). FIELD TRIP OPPORTUNITIES ARE EVERYWHERE.

TAKE A WALK DOWN A CREEK.

VISITING ANY HISTORICAL SITES, HOMES, MUSEUMS WHEN WE TRAVEL TO OTHER STATES, AND IN OUR HOME STATE, AS WELL.....THE WEALTH OF INFO IS ASTOUNDING, AND IT ENCOURAGES A PERSONAL INTEREST IN WHAT WOULD OTHERWISE BE DRY AS DUST HISTORY!

IT'S EASY TO COME UP WITH PROJECTS FOR YOUNGER, BUT WITH HIGH SCHOOLERS, I FOUND THE BENEFIT OF PULLING TOGETHER A HIGH SCHOOL LIT CLUB. WE MEET IN A BOOKSTORE WHICH MAKES THEM FEEL IT IS THEIR SPECIAL NIGHT OUT -- VERY IMPORTANT FOR TEENS. EACH STUDENT HAS A SPECIFIC JOB THEY GET A TURN AT AND COME PREPARED WITH WHEN ASSIGNED. FOR INSTANCE, SOMEONE IS BIOGRAPHER (TELLS BACKGROUND AND INCLUDES 5 INTERESTING FACTS NOT OTHERWISE KNOWN ABOUT THE AUTHOR); ANOTHER PERSON IS CONNECTOR (SHOWS HOW THE MESSAGE OF THE BOOK RELATES BACK IN HISTORY, OR ALSO MODERN TIMES); SOMEONE ELSE IS ILLUSTRATOR (THEY DRAW OR COME UP WITH A 3-D ITEM THAT DEPICTS SOMETHING INVOLVING THE STORY. THIS CAN DRAW IN SYMBOLISM AND OPEN DISCUSSION); DISCUSSION DIRECTOR (SOMEONE WHO "LEADS" THE DISCUSSION BY COMING PREPARED WITH 7-10 "FAT" QUESTIONS-- IE: QUESTIONS SUCH AS "WHICH CHARACTER DO YOU FIND YOURSELF IDENTIFYING WITH THE MOST AND WHY?", AND "IF YOU COULD RE-WRITE THE ENDING OF THE STORY, WHAT WOULD YOU CHANGE?", ETC. AND ANOTHER PERSON IS GEOGRAPHER AND MAKES A VISUAL MAP OF WHERE THE EVENTS IN THE STORY TAKE PLACE. IF THE GROUP IS LARGE (WHICH OURS IS, I SIMPLY HAVE 2 DISCUSSION DIRECTORS WHO EACH TAKE TURNS ASKING 5 QUESTIONS. THERE IS ALSO ROOM FOR SEVERAL ILLUSTRATORS.

THIS HAS BEEN A HUGE SUCCESS AND MEETS A GREAT NEED AMONG HOME SCHOOLED HIGH SCHOOL STUDENTS. I SELECT THE LITERATURE OFF THE CLASSICS/COLLEGE BOUND LISTS AND FACILITATE EACH MEETING AS AN ADULT "SUPERVISOR". BY SIMPLY ADVERTISING A HIGH SCHOOL LIT CLUB WITH THE BOOK SELECTIONS OVER OUR HOMESCHOOL SUPPORT GROUP EMAIL, I HAD 15 HOMESCHOOLERS SIGN UP -- AND THEY (AND THEIR PARENTS) ARE LOVING IT! SO AM I, AS I SIT IN ON THEIR DISCUSSIONS!

TRY MUMMIFYING A CHICKEN.

MAKING DIFFERENT PLAY DOUGHS, CREATING PROJECTS AND PUPPETS FROM
CONSTRUCTION PAPER, FELT BOARDS, AND COOKING

DUNKING COOKIES IN TEA AND COUNTING HOW LONG THE COOKIE TOOK UNTIL IT FELL
APART.

PLAYING SCRABBLE.

DRESSING UP.

ATTENDING THE RENAISSANCE FAIRE.

READING OUTSIDE IN THE SUN.

HATCHING BUTTERFLIES.

NATURE STUDY - OBSERVING FLORA AND FAUNA; DRAWING AN ILLUSTRATION AND
MAKING OBSERVATION NOTES IN OUR NATURE NOTEBOOKS; USING REFERENCE BOOKS TO
LEARN MORE ABOUT THE PLANT, INSECT, BIRD OR CREATURE.

POETRY & TEA-TIME - READING ALOUD ONE OR TWO POEMS; HAVE A HOT OR COLD
BEVERAGE AND A SNACK; LISTEN TO CLASSICAL MUSIC; SHARE OUR THOUGHTS AND
FEELINGS ABOUT THE POEM(S) AND/OR MUSIC.

WE MADE A MODEL OF THE EFFECTS OF THE FLOOD WATERS OF NOAH'S DAY. FILL A BABY FOOD JAR WITH DIRT FROM OUTSIDE. ABOUT HALF WAY. ADD WATER SHAKE AND WATCH LAYERS AND PARTICLES SETTLE OUT IN THE SLURRY.

WE SAY THE PLEDGE OF ALLEGIANCE EVERY MORNING TO STAY CIVIC MINDED.

WE PUT EXERCISE ON OUR DAILY SCHEDULE TO KEEP IN SHAPE AND WE ATTEND PARK DAY EVERY WEEK TO KEEP UP RELATIONSHIPS.

I KEEP A DAILY LOG OF ALL MY SON'S ATTITUDES, RESPONSES AND GENERAL WORK HABITS TO PUT IN A WEEKLY JOURNAL. THIS WAY I CAN LOOK BACK TO SEE PATTERNS AND MAKE CORRECTIONS WHERE NEEDED WHETHER IT'S WITH CURRICULUM OR HIS BEHAVIOR.

AT ONE TIME, THE HOMESCHOOLERS OF OUR CHURCH GATHERED TOGETHER ON FRIDAY MORNINGS TO POOL OUR TALENTS, SUCH AS MUSIC, ART, QUILTING AND OTHER HAND WORK, WOODWORKING PROJECTS, ETC. CO-OP'ING CAN BE FUN, ESPECIALLY WHEN THE CHILDREN ARE IN THE SAME AGE RANGE, AS IT CAN ALLOW THEM TO SEE OTHER FAMILIES DOING THE SAME THINGS AS THEY ARE. IT CAN ALSO FILL IN ANY 'GAPS' AND ALLOWS THE TEACHERS TO TEACH WHAT THEY HAVE A PASSION FOR, MAKING THE JOB OF TEACHING A BIT EASIER.

WE BELONG TO A CO-OP WHERE MY CHILDREN TAKE ELECTIVE-TYPE CLASSES (ARTS/CRAFTS, DANCE, PE, COOKING, HOMEMAKING, ETC.). IT HAS ENRICHED OUR HOMESCHOOL EXPERIENCE SO MUCH BECAUSE WE ARE WITH OTHER LIKE-MINDED HOMESCHOOLERS ONE DAY A WEEK AND MY CHILDREN GET TO MAKE AND DO FUN THINGS WITHOUT ME HAVING TO PREPARE IT ALL.

SPELLING BEES, WORD GAMES, CRANIUM GAMES.

BUILDING REPLICAS OF HISTORIC BUILDINGS OR MONUMENTS IN YOUR AREA. OUR KIDS HAD FUN MAKING REPLICAS OF CALIFORNIA MISSIONS.

DOING SERVICE PROJECTS LIKE HELPING OUT AT CHURCH AND BRINGING FOOD TO THE ELDERLY.

WE DID A UNIT STUDY ON THE HUMAN BODY, AND USED THE BODY BOOK (BY FRANK SCHAEFFER PUBLISHING), AND MADE AN OUTLINE OF OUR KIDS BODIES ON BUTCHER PAPER, AND AS THEY STUDIED EACH PART OF THEIR BODY, THEY COLORED THEM, CUT THEM OUT, AND PASTED THEM ONTO THE OUTLINES OF THEIR BODY. THEN WHEN THE UNIT WAS FINISHED, MY KIDS GOT TO HANG THEIR BODIES IN THEIR ROOMS FOR A QUARTER.

THE BEST ACTIVITIES ARE WHEN DAD GETS INVOLVED AND DOES ANY ACTIVITY WITH THE KIDS (DAD NEEDS TO DO THIS MORE.) A FAVORITE WAS MAKING SKELETONS (WE TRACED EACH CHILD ON BUTCHER PAPER) AND THEN LEARNING ABOUT BONES AND THEIR NAMES. WE ENJOY GOING ON NATURE HIKES AND EXPLORING. WE ONCE BROUGHT BACK SOME POND WATER AND THEN LOOKED AT DROPS UNDER A MICROSCOPE. IF YOU LET THE WATER "RIPEN" FOR A FEW DAYS THERE WILL BE ALL KINDS OF CRITTERS TO DISCOVER AND LEARN ABOUT.

OUR FAMILY VACATIONS INCLUDE NATIONAL & STATE PARKS, ETC. MOST OF OUR CHILDREN DO THE JR. RANGER PROGRAMS WHILE IN THE PARKS. IT IS A GREAT WAY TO LEARN ABOUT DIFFERENT THINGS IN HISTORY, GEOLOGY, SCIENCE, ETC. THEY COME AWAY FROM THE PARKS WITH A NEW INSIGHT ON THE PARK, AND A BADGE TO DISPLAY THEIR ACCOMPLISHMENTS.

WE'VE ENJOYED MAKING VOLCANOES, RAISING TADPOLES, MATH BY BAKING GOODIES, AND ESPECIALLY JUST BEING TOGETHER THROUGHOUT THE DAY! WE ALSO KEPT A WEATHER CHART FOR AN ENTIRE YEAR.

DAILY BIBLE READINGS.

BUILDING MODEL ROCKETS & CATAPULTS.

CAMPING AND MATH IN THE OUTDOORS.

RAISING ANIMALS -- DOGS, CATS, FISH, CHICKENS, DUCKS, GEESE, PIGS, GOATS

BUILDING A VIKING SHIP OUT OF WOOD, AND EGYPTIAN PYRAMID OUT OF SUGAR CUBES.

MATH CLUB -- HAVE SOME FRIENDS OVER ONCE OR TWICE A MONTH TO PLAY MATH GAMES AND WORK PUZZLES. THERE ARE PLENTY OF ACTIVITY IDEAS IN YOUR LIBRARY. LOOK FOR BOOKS BY MARILYN BURNS OR BRIAN BOLT, AND ALSO THE BOOK "FAMILY MATH" BY JEAN KERR STENMARK.

FIELD TRIPS WITH OUR LOCAL SUPPORT GROUP. IT'S WONDERFUL TO SEE THE KIDS LEARN ABOUT THE LOCAL BUSINESS, HAVING OUR CHILDREN TOGETHER AND FORMING FRIENDSHIPS WITH OTHERS WHO ARE LIKEMINDED AND FORMING FRIENDSHIPS MYSELF. THE SHARING OF IDEAS OF DIFFERENT HURDLES WE'VE COME UP AGAINST AND HOW WE GOT THROUGH/OVER THEM.

HERE IS A FAVORITE ACTIVITY WE DO:

HIKE THE CREATOR'S UNIVERSE: YOUR JOB IS TO SHRINK THE SOLAR SYSTEM DOWN TO 300 YARDS, AND THEN HIKE IT! FOR THE SUN, YOU WILL PLUNK DOWN A TENNIS BALL, THEN START WALKING. FOR THE PLANETS, BRING ALONG A FEW ROCKS TO SET IN PLACE. THE LENGTH OF THE PACE IS 1 1/2 FEET OR 18 INCHES. (WE JUST TOOK A BIG STEP). WE WENT TO LITTLE BUFFALO STATE PARK SO WE WOULD HAVE ENOUGH ROOM TO DO THIS.....YOU COULD GO TO AN OPEN FIELD, A FARMERS FIELD, A PARK OR SCHOOL TRACK OR FOOTBALL FIELD PERHAPS. 1. PLACE YOUR TENNIS BALL ON THE GROUND. IN SIX PACES DROP MERCURY. 2. WALK FIVE MORE PACES AND DROP VENUS. 3. WALK ANOTHER 4 PACES, EARTH, THIRD ROCK FROM THE SUN, PUT IT DOWN WITH SPECIAL CARE. 4. EIGHT MORE PACES TO MARS 5. 55 PACES TO JUPITER. 6. 65 PACES TO SATURN. 7. 144 PACES TO URANUS. 8. 163 PACES TO NEPTUNE 9. 140 PACES TO THE LAST PLANET PLUTO.

NOW, LOOK OVER YOUR SHOULDER. THIS IS THE SOLAR SYSTEM OUR HEAVENLY FATHER CREATED FOR US, FROM PLUTO LOOKING IN. AS YOU STRAIN TO SEE YOUR TENNIS BALL SUN (300 YARDS AWAY), ONE LESSON OF THIS HIKE OUGHT TO START COMING INTO FOCUS.....WHAT IS IT? NOTHING.......HUGE LENGTHY GOBS OF IT. THINK ABOUT IT. YOU'VE JUST MODELED OUR SOLAR SYSTEM BY WALKING 300 YARDS AND DROPPING A FEW LITTLE ROCKS ALONG THE WAY. AND OUR SOLAR SYSTEM IS A CROWDED PLACE! BEYOND PLUTO, IT GETS LONELY OUT THERE. USING THIS SAME SCALE, IT IS 1,200 MORE MILES TO THE NEAREST STAR- AND THERE ISN'T EVEN A PLANET EN ROUTE! *CONSIDER ALL THE WONDROUS THINGS HE MADE AND START TO REALIZE THAT ETERNITY LITERALLY MEANS "TO TIME OUT OF MIND" (THIS LESSON WAS ADAPTED FROM THE AWARD WINNING KLUTZ BOOKS)

MIDDLE AGES, ESPECIALLY CASTLES, WE CHECKED BOOKS OUT OF THE LOCAL LIBRARY READ THEM AND FOLLOWED UP WITH MORE BOOKS ON AREAS OF INTEREST ALSO SEVERAL HAD ACTIVITIES IN THEM WHICH WE DID. EG MAKING COSTUMES, SCENTS, WEAVING, COOKING ETC. WE ALSO HAD A BOOK WHICH WENT THROUGH THE BUILDING OF A CASTLE INCLUDING DIMENSIONS SO WE MEASURED EVERYTHING OUT TO GIVE A CLEARER PICTURE OF JUST HOW BIG THEY WERE.

POSTCARD SWAP WITH OTHER FAMILIES FROM US AND ABROAD. LOCATED FAMILIES AND SIGNED UP FOR SWAPS ON YAHOO GROUPS.

PARTICIPATING IN CIVIL WAR RE-ENACTMENTS.

TO START OUR HOMESCHOOL YEAR OFF WITH A "BANG," WE ALWAYS WHACK AT A PINATA AND LET BALLOONS GO WITH A SMALL MESSAGE ATTACHED, HOPING FOR A LETTER IN RETURN.

ANY SCIENCE PROJECT THAT MAKES A MESS, ESPECIALLY MAKING OOOZE (SLIME) AND DISSECTING OWL PELLETS THIS YEAR WAS A REAL HIT!

USING THE INTERNET TO LOOK UP "REAL LIFE" PHOTOS OF THINGS WE ARE STUDYING IN REGARDS TO GEOGRAPHY AND HISTORY. THIS MAY SEEM LIKE A NO-BRAINER, BUT I'VE TALKED TO OTHERS AND THEY JUST DON'T DO THIS. FOR EXAMPLE, WHEN READING SECRET OF THE ANDES, WE LOOKED UP PERU ONLINE AND FOUND A GREAT PHOTO DOCUMENTARY ON THE COUNTRY AND ITS HISTORY. SUPER BENEFICIAL!!

BUILDING A VOLCANO IN SANDPIT, ADDING RED FOOD COLORING, WITH VINEGAR AND BAKING SODA. USING CHEAP SHAVING FOAM TO ILLUSTRATE MOUNTAINS, VALLEY, PLATEAUS, PEAKS ETC. DONE OUTSIDE ON A SUMMERS DAY, MADE FOR A FUN AFTERNOON, WHEN DONE WE ADDED OUR TOGS AND THE HOSE!

WE HAVE A FALL FUN DAY EVERY SEPTEMBER. WE BOB FOR APPLES, BUILD SCARECROWS, GUESSTIMATE M&MS IN A JAR, GUESSTIMATE PUMPKIN SEEDS IN PUMPKINS, TIE DONUTS TO STRINGS AND HANG THEM ON TREE BRANCHES TRYING TO EAT THEM OFF THE STRING WITHOUT USING OUR HANDS, ETC. ANY FUN IDEA IS GREAT! WE INVITE OUR FRIENDS AND HAVE A BLAST! THE CLOSEST GUESSER WINS THE M&MS, PUMPKINS AND SEEDS FOR COOKING.

ONE THING I'VE DONE FOR ELEVEN YEARS AND HAVEN'T STOPPED (EVEN THOUGH MY OLDEST IS 15) IS READING OUT LOUD TO MY KIDS. WE ARE ALWAYS READING A BOOK (SOMETIMES EVEN TWO), YEAR ROUND. WE USUALLY READ FOR AT LEAST 30 MINUTES, SOMETIMES AN HOUR IF EVERYONE IS REALLY CAUGHT UP IN IT. I LET THE KIDS COLOR, PLAY WITH LEGOS, DO ART, ETC. WHILE I READ IF THEY WANT, AS LONG AS THEY LISTEN. THAT HELPS LITTLE ONES. WE'VE READ SO MANY WONDERFUL STORIES AND SPENT SUCH WONDERFUL TIMES (AND HAD SO MANY INTERESTING DISCUSSIONS) THAT I WOULDN'T TRADE THAT FOR ANYTHING. WE STILL READ MOST EVERY DAY.

ADOPT-A-GRANDMA/GRANDPA THROUGH OUR LOCAL ASSISTED LIVING FACILITY COLLECTING ORAL HISTORIES FROM THE ADOPTED GRANDMAS AND GRANDPAS AND THEN COMPILING THEM INTO A BOUND BOOK FOR EACH OF THE RESIDENTS (FACILITY PROVIDED FUNDING FOR PROJECT)

EACH YEAR WE HAVE CHRISTMAS SCHOOL. EVERYTHING "NORMALLY" DONE DURING SCHOOL IS PUT ON HOLD FOR A FEW WEEKS AND WE WILL DEVOTE OUR TIME TO VARIOUS HOLIDAY TASKS. WE DO A LOT OF READING, WE USUALLY INTENSELY STUDY A COUNTRY AND THEIR HOLIDAY CUSTOMS, AND WE DO PLENTY OF CRAFTS AND BAKING. WE ALSO ENJOY DOING MORE SERVANT PROJECTS DURING THIS TIME. OUR FAMILY DEVOTIONS USUALLY CENTER AROUND A NEW BOOK OR THE JESSE TREE. IT IS A TIME OF WONDERFUL FAMILY FELLOWSHIP.

STUDYING HISTORY BY WEARING CLOTHES FROM THE TIME PERIOD, MAKING CRAFTS, EATING FOOD, AND READING BOOKS ALOUD...ALL FROM THE TIME PERIOD. OUR FAVORITE PROJECT WAS WHEN WE MADE A CASTLE TOTALLY OUT OF CARD BOARD BOXES AND A HOT GLUE GUN. IT WAS HUGE!(ABOUT 4FT TALL!) IT HAD THREE FLOORS WITH A WORKING DRAWBRIDGE AND TOILETS EMPTYING INTO THE MOAT. WE MADE WOODEN FLOORS WITH PAINTED POPSICLE STICKS. WE FOUND PEOPLE IN BOOKS ON CASTLES, REDUCED THEM TO THE SCALE OF OUR CASTLE AND COLORED THEM. THEY LOOKED GREAT! WE MADE ALL THE FURNITURE WITH POPSICLE STICKS AND COLORED FELT. IT WAS AN AWESOME SIGHT!

WE HAVE UNIT CELEBRATIONS AT THE END OF EACH OF OUR 4 UNITS EACH YEAR. WE MAKE DISPLAY BOARDS, COSTUMES, DISPLAY OUR PROJECTS ETC.... WE INVITE SEVERAL GUESTS OVER AND HAVE A MEAL RELATED TO THE TIME PERIOD AND ALLOW THE GUESTS TO CRITIQUE THE WORK THE CHILDREN HAVE COMPLETED. IT IS THE HIGHLIGHT OF OUR STUDIES! THE CHILDREN REALLY ENJOY IT! WE HAVE AWESOME PICTURES FROM OUR CELEBRATION LAST NIGHT, INCLUDING A LIFE SIZE HOMEMADE MUMMY, DEATH MASK, HUGE TERAHS FAMILY TREE, CHILDREN DRESSED AS ISRAELITES, AND EVEN MY SON THE PHAROAH COMPLETE WITH SHAVED HEAD!

HISTORY CLUB - MEETING WITH A FEW OTHER FAMILIES ONCE A WEEK TO DISCOVER AN HISTORIC TIME PERIOD, CULMINATING IN A DINNER/PARTY SET IN THAT TIME. COOPERATIVE - FOR TWO YEARS, WE HAVE BEEN MEMBERS OF A COOPERATIVE THAT MEETS ONCE PER WEEK, FOR GROUP LEARNING AND PLAYING. CURRENTLY 10 FAMILIES MEET, AND IT'S AN EXCELLENT OPPORTUNITY FOR OUR CHILDREN TO WORK ON GROUP PROJECTS, SOCIALIZE AND PARTICIPATE IN PROJECTS THAT ARE NOT EASY TO DO AT HOME.

I LIKE SURPRISING THE KIDS AND PACKING OUR BOOKS TO A COFFEE SHOP, OR THE BEACH. THEN READ THEM A GOOD BOOK, OR GO TO A MUSEUM OR ART GALLERY, MAYBE A GLASS BLOWING STORE. THEY GET NEW IDEAS FOR THEIR ESSAY FOR THE DAY, GET TO MEET NEW PEOPLE, AND GET KNOCKED OUT OF THE RUT OF BEING AT HOME ALL THE TIME. SOMETIMES WE TAKE SMALL MUSICAL INSTRUMENTS WITH US AND TRY OUR HAND AT THEM WHILE OUT. IF THE CHILDREN GET EXPOSED TO THE WORLD IN A POSITIVE WAY, THEY MIGHT FIND SOMETHING THAT THEY WANT TO DO WITH THEIR LIFE WHILE WE ARE OUT EXPLORING. THEY HAVE A GREAT SENSE OF ADVENTURE AND I'LL SURE MISS THEM WHEN THEY ARE GONE.

MAKING A PINHOLE CAMERA AND DEVELOPING THE FILM OURSELVES.

HANDS ON SCIENCE IS ONE OF THE FUNNEST. YOU DON'T HAVE TO COAX THE KIDS INTO DOING IT. THEY CAN'T WAIT TO DIG IN. I HAVE TWO BOYS, SO ANYTIME THEY CAN LIGHT SOMETHING ON FIRE OR BLOW SOMETHING UP, THEY'RE ELATED! THE BOOK "BACKYARD BALLISTICS" IS A GREAT SOURCE OF IDEAS.

WE HAD "HOMESCHOOL FUN DAY" IN THE TOWN WE LIVED IN PRIOR TO OUR MOVE. ONCE A MONTH, A GROUP OF HOMESCHOOLERS IN THE SAME CHURCH FELLOWSHIP WOULD GET TOGETHER WITH OUR KIDS AND DO HANDS ON ACTIVITIES AS WELL AS BOOK REPORTS, PROGRESS REPORTS, ESSAYS, SPEECHES, ETC. IT GAVE THE KIDS THE CHANCE TO SHOW OFF THEIR WORK TO THEIR PEERS, LEARN A NEW SKILL (OUR FAVORITES WERE PIE MAKING, CAKE DECORATING, AND SEWING PILLOWS ...CAN YOU TELL WE HAVE GIRLS? THE BOYS ENJOYED THESE CLASSES TOO, BTW.), AND RUN AND PLAY WITH KIDS WHO WERE LEARNING AT HOME LIKE THEY WERE.

EVERY YEAR OUR LOCAL SUPPORT GROUP PUTS ON AN INTERNATIONAL FAIR. FAMILIES (OR ANY GROUPING OF KIDS) GET TOGETHER AND STUDY A COUNTRY, MAKE A PRESENTATION BOARD, AND PUT ON A 5 MINUTE PRESENTATION OF ANY SONGS, DANCES, OR OTHER ACTIVITIES THEY LEARNED ABOUT (COMPLETE WITH COSTUME IF DESIRED). LAST TIME WE STUDIED ISRAEL, CONCENTRATING ON THE JEWISH ISRAELITES, AND LEARNED ABOUT MANY JEWISH CUSTOMS AND FESTIVALS, LEARNED A JEWISH DANCE, AND MADE CHALLAH AND MATZAH TO SHARE WITH THE WHOLE GROUP. WE HAD A BLAST AND WILL STUDY THE ARAB ISRAELITES NEXT YEAR.

WHILE STUDYING ANIMALS, WE MAKE SEVERAL TRIPS TO LOCAL ZOOS AND TOOK PICTURES OF THE ANIMALS WE WERE STUDYING AS WELL AS A CLOSE-UP PICTURE OF THE INFORMATION PLAQUE(S) FOR EACH ANIMAL. WE THEN MADE OUR OWN INFORMATION BOOK (AKA. SCRAPBOOK) OF THE PICTURES AND INFORMATION. IT PROVIDED LEARNING, REVIEW, PHYSICAL EXERCISE (OUR ZOO IS ON THE SIDE OF A MOUNTAIN), CRAFT, AND GREAT MOTHER/SON CONNECTION TIME!

OUR ALL-TIME FAVORITE ACTIVITY HAS BEEN PARTICIPATING IN THE "YOUNG EAGLES FLYING PROGRAM". THIS PROGRAM IS USUALLY OFFERED ON A SATURDAY MORNING AT LOCAL SMALL AIRPORTS ALL ACROSS THE COUNTRY. THE PROGRAM OFFERS A 1/2-HOUR "FLIGHT SCHOOL" GIVEN BY A LOCAL FLIGHT SCHOOL INSTRUCTOR AND THEN PAIRS UP 1-4 CHILDREN WITH A PILOT WHO TAKES THE CHILDREN FOR A PLANE-RIDE (USUALLY FOR @ 30-45 MINUTES). IN OUR AREA, THEY TAKE OFF FROM OUR LOCAL AIRPORT AND TRAVEL 15-20 MILES TO ANOTHER, LARGER AIRPORT WHERE THEY LAND, THE KIDS TRADE SEATS AND THEN THEY RETURN. THE VERY FIRST PLANE RIDE YIELDED AN EXTREMELY EXCITED 10-YEAR-OLD, WHO DECLARED FOR THE FIRST TIME EVER THAT HE KNEW WHAT HE WANTED TO DO WHEN HE GROWS UP!! HE WENT ON TO TELL ME THAT IN ORDER TO BE A PILOT HE NEEDED TO LEARN A LOT ABOUT MATH AND SCIENCE - AND HE WAS READY TO DO WHATEVER IT TOOK TO MAKE THIS HAPPEN!! EVEN MORE REMARKABLE TO US WAS THE FACT THAT THIS CHILD HAS STRUGGLED WITH SERIOUS DYSLEXIA AND HAD PREVIOUSLY AVOIDED THESE SUBJECTS LIKE THE PLAGUE! SINCE THIS REVELATION, HE ALWAYS KEEPS HIS GOAL OF BECOMING A PILOT ONE DAY AS A ABSOLUTE MOTIVATOR FOR ANYTHING HE NEEDS TO CONQUER!! AS OF NOW, SOME TWO YEARS AND THREE PLANE RIDES LATER, (TWO RIDES WERE WITH ONLY HE AND THE PILOT - WHO LET HIM TAKE THE CONTROLS FOR A FEW MINUTES!!) HE AND HIS OLDER BROTHER HAVE NOT ONLY PICKED OUT THEIR FIRST PLANE, BUT HAVE BEGUN MAKING PLANS FOR HOW THEY WILL MAKE IT HAPPEN! THIS INCLUDES A PLAN FOR GETTING THE FUNDS TO TAKE FLYING LESSONS AND WHAT KIND OF BUSINESS THEY WANT TO BUILD AFTER THEY GET THEIR LICENSES! WHAT A GREAT BLESSING THIS HAS BEEN FOR ALL OF US - CHECK IT OUT AT YOUR LOCAL SMALL AIRPORT!

MY DAUGHTER HAS DONE MANY VOLUNTEER ACTIVITIES DURING OUR HOMESCHOOLING YEARS. SHE IS IN THE EIGHTH GRADE THIS YEAR. FOR ONE YEAR, SHE SPENT ONE DAY A WEEK AT OUR LOCAL ELEMENTARY SCHOOL HELPING IN THE LIBRARY AND GUIDANCE OFFICE. ANOTHER YEAR SHE SPENT 6 MONTHS WITH "CITY YEAR" YOUNG HEROES VOLUNTEERING AROUND OUR CAPITAL CITY WITH CLEAN UP AND BEAUTIFICATION PROJECTS. THIS YEAR SHE WILL WORK WITH THE ACTIVITIES DIRECTOR AT A LOCAL ASSISTED LIVING FACILITY. I FEEL THESE VOLUNTEER OPPORTUNITIES HELP MY DAUGHTER TO FEEL LESS "STUCK" AT HOME. THESE ACTIVITIES HELP WITH SELF ESTEEM AS WELL AS TEACHING HER TO BE AN ACTIVE MEMBER OF OUR COMMUNITY. SHE RECEIVED THE "PRESIDENTS AWARD FOR VOLUNTEERISM" FOR HER WORK WITH CITY YEAR. MY DAUGHTER IS VERY PROUD OF HER VOLUNTEER WORK AND I WOULD HIGHLY RECOMMEND THAT OTHER HOMESCHOOLING FAMILIES LOOK FOR VOLUNTEER OPPORTUNITIES FOR THEIR CHILDREN.

WE FORMED A SHAKESPEARE CLASS WITH 4 HOMESCHOOLING FAMILIES. ONE OF THE MOMS HAD HER MASTERS IN ENGLISH LITERATURE AND WAS WILLING TO TAKE ON THE TASK OF TEACHING SHAKESPEARE TO A GROUP OF 8 TEENAGERS. IN LIEU OF CASH PAYMENT FOR EACH CLASS EACH FAMILY GIVES THE TEACHER A DINNER. SHE HAS A NEWLY ADOPTED BABY AND NEEDED DINNERS MUCH MORE THAN SHE DID MONEY! WE HAVE ALSO, GIVEN A DINNER TO THE HOSTESS FOR ALLOWING US TO USE HER HOME. THE CHILDREN HAVE LOVED IT AND PERFORMED ONE PLAY ALREADY. OF COURSE, THE PARENTS ARE THRILLED THAT THEIR CHILDREN ARE LOVING SHAKESPEARE AND GETTING THIS WONDERFUL EDUCATION IN A CHRISTIAN ENVIRONMENT. THIS COULD BE APPLIED TO ANY SUBJECT AND IN FACT WE ARE THINKING ABOUT ADDING SPANISH FOR NEXT YEAR!

MAKING MAPS.. FROM STORIES WE READ. CURRENTLY WE ARE WORKING ON PADDLE TO THE SEA, AND ALL THE CHILDREN LOVE TO MAKE THE MAP OF PADDLE'S JOURNEY. WE MADE A MAP OF CHRISTOPHER COLUMBUS'S FIRST VOYAGE.. WE MAKE HUGE MAPS.. AND HAVE ALL THE CHILDREN SIT AROUND THE MAP TO COLOR AND RECORD STATES/COUNTRIES/OCEANS/RIVERS ETC. WEEKS)

THE MOST FUN (MOST WORK, TOO) THING WE EVER DID WAS SOMETHING WE AFFECTIONATELY CALLED "INDIANA HISTORY BY TRAVELING AROUND". WE SPENT A YEAR (WELL, ALMOST A YEAR AND A HALF) STUDYING IN HISTORY WITH ANOTHER FAMILY. EVERY OTHER FRIDAY WE WOULD TAKE A FIELD TRIP. SOMETIMES THEY WERE ONE DAY ONLY (NEARBY), SOME WERE AS LONG AS FIVE DAYS (TO A DISTANT REGION OF THE STATE). THE MOMS SPLIT THE STATE IN HALF (ONE GREW UP IN THE NORTH, THE OTHER IN THE SOUTH) AND ALTERNATED FIELD TRIPS SO EACH PERSON WAS ONLY PLANNING ONE TRIP PER MONTH. WE WOULD HAVE LIKED TO STUDY CHRONOLOGICALLY, BUT WOUND UP HAVING TO IGNORE CHRONOLOGY AND JUST STUDY GEOGRAPHICALLY. WE WERE ABLE TO COMPENSATE SOMEWHAT BY HAVING EACH KID KEEP A TIMELINE ALL YEAR. THE FAMILY PLANNING THE NEXT TRIP COULD GIVE READING ASSIGNMENTS, ETC. IN BETWEEN AND WE FOUND SOME WONDERFUL RESOURCES AT THE LIBRARY.

SOME THINGS WE FOUND TO BE IMPORTANT WERE:

1. IT WORKS BEST IF THE TWO FAMILIES CAN FIT IN ONE VEHICLE - MOM TIME IS CRUCIAL. IT ALSO ALLOWED WHOEVER WASN'T DRIVING TO NAVIGATE AND/OR READ ABOUT WHATEVER WAS COMING NEXT. IN OUR CASE, ONE OF THE DADS WAS ABLE TO GO ON MANY OF OUR OUTINGS AS WELL (A BIG BONUS).
2. IT IS VERY IMPORTANT THAT THE TWO FAMILIES ARE SIMILARLY "WIRED". THAT IS, THEY HAVE SIMILAR TOLERANCE FOR AMOUNT OF ACTIVITY, TYPES OF ACCOMMODATIONS, MEAL PLANS, COST, ETC. 3. IT DOESN'T MATTER WHAT THE BOOK SAYS, CALL TO VERIFY ALL TIMES AND COSTS. IT IS VERY FRUSTRATING TO HUSTLE TO ARRIVE SOMEWHERE AT A SPECIFIC TIME ONLY TO FIND OUT THEY DO THINGS DIFFERENTLY NOW! 4. DON'T BE AFRAID TO ASK. WE GOT SOME REALLY OUTSTANDING TOURS OF PLACES YOU AREN'T SUPPOSED TO BE ABLE TO GO OR CAN ONLY GO IF YOU ARE A SCHOOL OR WHATEVER BECAUSE WE GOT QUITE BRAZEN ABOUT ASKING SPECIFICALLY FOR WHAT WE WERE INTERESTED IN STUDYING. MANY PEOPLE REALLY ENJOYED HELPING US LEARN OUR STATE'S HISTORY THIS WAY (OF COURSE WE WERE SOMETIMES TOLD "NO" IN A LESS THAN GRACIOUS WAY, TOO). 5. KEEP THE KIDS ACCOUNTABLE. WE DID THIS BY HAVING THEM MAKE THE TIME LINE MENTIONED ABOVE, COLOR IN ALL COUNTIES VISITED ON A STATE MAP, AND KEEP A NOTEBOOK/SCRAPBOOK OF ALL TRIPS (DETAIL REQUIRED DEPENDED ON THE AGE OF THE STUDENT). IT'S BEST (BUT NOT ALWAYS POSSIBLE IF YOU TOLERATE A HIGH LEVEL OF ACTIVITY) TO DO THE NOTEBOOK THE SAME DAY AS THE EVENT. THIS IS ESPECIALLY TRUE ON MULTI-DAY TRIPS.

WE LIKE TO RAISE ANY KIND OF ANIMALS, ESPECIALLY INSECTS FROGS, LIZARDS, ETC. WE ALSO ENJOY LOOKING AT THINGS UNDER A MICROSCOPE.

I THINK THE MOST FUN ONE WOULD HAVE TO BE WHEN MY SON BUILT AN PORTABLE EXTERNAL HARD DRIVE FOR THE COMPUTER. HE USED AN OLD METAL BOX AND EXTRA SPARE COMPUTER PARTS. IT WAS A PROJECT HE WORKED ON WITH HIS DAD. HE'S TAKEN THIS EVERYWHERE.

I'M A BIG FAN OF ART....HISTORICAL CONTEXT, ARCHITECTURE, HISTORIC LANDMARKS, MEMORIALS, TRENDS. YOU CAN USE ART AS A BASIS FOR JOURNALING, BIOGRAPHIES, HISTORICAL AND BIBLICAL EVENTS, DESIGNING AND LANDSCAPING...AS WELL AS AN CREATIVE OUTLET. MY FAVORITE PROJECT TO DATE HAD BEEN OUR MODEL OF THE HUMAN BODY WHEN I HAD 1ST GRADERS-WE DREW THEIR OUTLINES ON BACK OF WRAPPING PAPER, GLUED THAT TO CARDBOARD THEN DO A SMALL LESSON ON THE BRAIN, THE DIGESTIVE SYSTEM, HEART, LUNGS, ETC. WE HEADED TO OUR 'BODIES' AFTER EACH LESSON... STRINGING CHEERIOS AND FRUIT LOOPS ON YARN TO REPRESENT THE SPINE, RED AND BLUE RIBBONS TO SHOW HOW BLOOD TRAVELS TO THE FEET AND HANDS THEN BACK AGAIN, CUT OUT HEART, LUNGS, BONES, BE CREATIVE AND DON'T FORGET... DA VINCI, MADAME CURIE, DR. WILLIAM HARVEY AND OTHER PIONEERS IN UNDERSTANDING OF HOW THE BODY WORKS.

WE FOCUS ON SCIENCE DURING THE SUMMER MONTHS WHEN WEATHER IS NICE (TO CATCH UP!). OUR FAVORITE ACTIVITY IS FOSSIL HUNTING. IT IS MIND-BENDING TO HOLD SOMETHING IN YOUR HAND THAT WAS BURIED DURING THE TIME OF THE FLOOD, LEAVING THESE TRACKS BEHIND. YOU LEARN A LOT ABOUT HUNTING, IDENTIFYING, SORTING, AND OTHER ACTIVITIES AS WELL. WE ARE BLESSED TO BE NEAR GLEN ROSE, TX AND THE DINOSAUR TRACKS THERE.

ANOTHER EASY AND EYE-OPENING ACTIVITY WE DID WAS TO COUNT OUT A MILLION GRAINS OF RICE INTO A DISHPAN. WE DIDN'T ACTUALLY COUNT THEM ALL OUT; WE MEASURED 1/4 CUP, COUNTED THOSE GRAINS, THEN MEASURED THE REST IN A ONE-CUP MEASURE. IT IS AMAZING TO SEE HOW MUCH A MILLION REALLY IS!

WHEN IT IS COLD OUTSIDE, WE SIT AROUND THE FIRE DRINKING HOT CHOCOLATE AND READ STORIES AND POEMS AND BIBLE SCRIPTURE. THIS IS A VERY ATYPICAL "TRADITIONAL SCHOOL ROOM SETTING" AND THAT IS WHY MY KIDS LOVE IT. SOMETIMES THEY LOOK WAY TOO COMFORTABLE TO POSSIBLE BE LEARNING ANYTHING, HA! BUT IT'S AMAZING WHAT THEY RETAIN WHEN IT SEEMS FUN. ALSO ON WARM DAYS IN THE SPRING AND FALL, WE GO OUTSIDE ON A NATURE WALK WHILE THE "REAL WORLD" IS STUCK BEHIND A DESK SOMEWHERE LOOKING OUT THE WINDOW. GOD HAS REALLY BLESSED US WITH THIS AWESOME OPPORTUNITY AND RESPONSIBILITY.

WE HAVE SCHOOL IN OUR DINING ROOM, SO WE PUT A BIRD FEEDER OUTSIDE OUR DINING ROOM WINDOW. WE MADE A TALLY SHEET OF BIRDS THAT ARE NATIVE TO TENNESSEE. SO EACH TIME ONE OF THESE BIRDS CAME TO VISIT OUR BIRD FEEDER, WE WOULD MARK IT ON OUR SHEET. WHEN A "STRANGER" WOULD COME TO VISIT THE FEEDER, WE HAD THE OPPORTUNITY TO RESEARCH WHAT KIND OF BIRD IT WAS. WE NOTICED PATTERNS IN SOME BIRDS BEHAVIOR AS WELL. SUCH AS WHEN A FEMALE CARDINAL WOULD COME TO EAT, MOST OF THE TIME THE MALE CAME FIRST AND "CLEARED" OUT ANY BIRDS THAT MIGHT BE DANGEROUS. SOMETIMES WE WOULD SEE HER COME WITHOUT THE MALE AND WOULD THINK OUR THEORY WAS WRONG ABOUT HIS PROTECTING HER. BUT WE WOULD LOOK AROUND AND SEE HIM UP ON THE POWER LINE "KEEPING WATCH" OVER HIS LADY.

I LIKE WATCHING "APPLIED MATH" IN THE KITCHEN WITH DOUBLED RECIPES, ETC. MY BOYS ENJOY CONQUERING REAL-WORLD SITUATIONS BASED ON THE THINGS THEY HAVE LEARNED IN SCHOOL. IT GIVES THEM A FEELING OF ACCOMPLISHMENT AND HELPS THEM UNDERSTAND THE PURPOSE OF THEIR STUDIES.

EVERYTHING WE DO SEEMS TO REVOLVE AROUND SCHOOL, SO MY KIDS HERE ME SAY ALL THE TIME THAT SCHOOL IS LIFE AND LIFE IS SCHOOL...YOU SHOULD BE LEARNING ALL THE TIME! SHOPPING, FIELD TRIPS, CAMPING TRIPS, ETC ALWAYS HAVE SOMETHING TO LEARN FROM. THE BIBLE DEUTERONOMY 11 TELLS US TO TEACH OUR CHILDREN AS WE SIT AT HOME, WALK ALONG THE PATH, LIE DOWN, OR GET UP. IT IS AMAZING HOW MANY TIMES I CAN QUOTE A VERSE OR PASSAGE FROM THE BIBLE, AND/OR SOMETHING THAT WE'VE LEARNED IN SCHOOL.

WE DO A LOT OF READING ALOUD AS A FAMILY. WE USUALLY SPEND OUR EVENINGS READING AND PLAYING INSTEAD OF WATCHING TELEVISION. WE HAVE SUCH AN INNER BOND WITH ONE ANOTHER BECAUSE OF THE BOOKS WE'VE READ. WE OFTEN RELATE BACK TO WHAT ONE OF THE CHARACTERS WE READ ABOUT FELT, DID OR WENT THROUGH. ONE OF THE FAVORITE PLACES FOR MY CHILDREN TO GO TO IS THE LIBRARY AND THE BOOKS STORES. DON'T GET ME WRONG...THEY ARE KIDS AND THEY LOVE TO GO TO THE TOY STORE, BUT THEY KNOW THAT THEY HAVE A HIGHER CHANCE OF COAXING ME INTO BUYING A BOOK THAN THEY HAVE OF COAXING ME TO BUY A TOY - SO THAT MAY BE PART OF THE INCENTIVE. BUT I WILL OFTEN FIND THEM PERUSING THROUGH BOOKS WHEN THEY ARE LEFT ALONE FOR A BIT. WE'VE USED SEVERAL BOOKS TO HELP US CHOOSE FAMILY BOOKS/AUTHORS TO READ: HONEY FOR A CHILD'S HEART, BOOKS CHILDREN LOVE, THE BOOK TREE, AND THE READ-ALOUD HANDBOOK. ANOTHER INCENTIVE FOR READING IS THAT MOST OF THE TIME, I WON'T ALLOW THEM TO WATCH A MOVIE UNLESS THEY HAVE FIRST READ THE BOOK. ONLY ONCE HAVE THEY FOUND THE MOVIE TO BE BETTER THAN THE BOOK AND ONLY TWICE HAVE THEY FOUND THE MOVIE TO BE CLOSE TO AS GOOD AS THE BOOK. AND THROUGHOUT THE MOVIE, THEY PICK OUT THE INCONSISTENCIES BETWEEN THE BOOK AND THE MOVIE. MOST OF THE TIME I DO NOT USE A COMPREHENSION GUIDE WHILE WE READ BECAUSE I WANT IT TO BE FUN, BUT IF THERE ARE THINGS THAT I NEED TO ADDRESS BECAUSE THEY ARE INCONSISTENT WITH GOD'S WORD THEN I ADDRESS IT AND WE TALK ABOUT IT. USUALLY THEY ARE TALKING AND TALKING ABOUT THE BOOK WITH ME OR EACH OTHER AND SO I KNOW HOW MUCH THEY UNDERSTOOD WHILE WE WERE READING. I PICK BOOKS THAT ARE OF ALL AGE RANGES BECAUSE OF THE AGE RANGE OF CHILDREN THAT I HAVE (INFANT — 12 YEARS OLD). I ALSO ENCOURAGE MY OLDER CHILDREN TO READ TO MY YOUNGER CHILDREN. ONCE THEY HAVE GONE THROUGH A BIT OF PHONICS AND ARE READING EARLY READER BOOKS, I HAVE THEM START READING TO THEIR YOUNGER SIBLINGS. THIS GIVES THEM PRACTICE AND ENTERTAINS THE YOUNGER ONES WHILE I GET SOMETHING ELSE DONE (A 3-FOLD BENEFIT).

A THANKSGIVING PARTY WITH OUR SUPPORT GROUP WAS ONE OF MY FAVORITE ACTIVITIES BECAUSE IT INCLUDED ALL AGES AND EVERYONE ENJOYED IT. YEARS AGO WHEN WE WERE ALL NEW TO HOMESCHOOLING WE HELD A PARTY IN A LOCAL STATE PARK. THE KIDS DRESSED IN HOMEMADE COSTUMES AS EITHER PILGRIMS OR INDIANS. SOME OF US ADULTS DRESSED UP TOO. I ASSIGNED EVERY TEEN A GAME TO TEACH AND PLAY WITH THE YOUNGER KIDS. EVERYONE BROUGHT A FINGER FOOD MADE FROM A TRADITIONAL THANKSGIVING FOOD (POPCORN BALLS, CRANBERRY BREAD, ETC.) A FEW CHILDREN GAVE SMALL PRESENTATIONS (POEMS, REPORTS) RELATED TO THANKSGIVING. THAT DAY GOD BLESSED US WITH A PERFECT FALL DAY. THE LITTLE ONES AND THE TEENS ALL HAD A GREAT TIME.

THIS MAY SEEM SIMPLE, BUT CONSTRUCTING PLAY HOUSES OUT OF POPSICLE STICKS. THE OTHER ONE IS MORE FOR MEMORIES SAKE. MAKING HAND PAINTED PLATES WITH THE DATES ON THEM AND ALSO HAND AND FOOT PRINTS. MY ONE SON BUILT A BRIDGE OUT OF STICKS A FEW YEARS BACK AND STILL HAS IT.

IN GENERAL, LET YOUR FAMILY LEARN FIRST-HAND WHAT "DELIGHT-DRIVEN LEARNING" MEANS. LET YOUR CHILD'S INTEREST DRIVE YOU TO EXCITING LEARNING OPPORTUNITIES. IF YOUR KID LOVES AIRPLANES, LET HIM DRAW THEM AND/OR MAKE MODELS WHILE YOU LEARN ABOUT THE BERNOULLI PRINCIPLE. IF YOUR CHILD LOVES SCIENCE-FICTION, USE THAT TO TEACH HIM ASTRONOMY. REMEMBER THOSE WORKBOOKS WE USED IN PUBLIC SCHOOL? HOW MUCH OF IT DO YOU REALLY REMEMBER? LET YOU CHILD LEARN BY DOING WHAT INTERESTS HIM. HE WILL DEVELOP A LOVE OF LEARNING THAT WILL BE THE FOUNDATION FOR A LIFETIME OF KNOWLEDGE.

MY ABSOLUTE FAVORITE AT-HOME HOME SCHOOL ACTIVITY IS PRETTY SIMPLE: MAKING A GINGERBREAD HOUSE FROM ROYAL ICING (PURCHASED FROM A BAKERY) AND GRAHAM CRACKERS! WE'VE HAD YEARS OF FUN DOING THIS, AND EVERYONE IN THE FAMILY GETS INCREDIBLY CREATIVE. WE'VE DONE THIS WITH OTHER HOME SCHOOL FAMILIES, FRIENDS AND NEIGHBORS - INVITING THEM TO JOIN US! ALL WE ASK IS THAT EVERYONE BRING ONE SACK OF CANDY. IT'S A FUN, BONDING TIME, WHEN ALL OF US SHARE WHAT WE'VE BROUGHT AND CREATE BEAUTIFUL THINGS!

WATCHING CATERPILLARS TURN INTO BUTTERFLIES, RAISING TADPOLES INTO FROGS.

FOR AGES 8+, THE LEWIS & CLARK ADVENTURE GAME. THIS TAKES YOU ON AN EXPEDITION FROM ST. LOUIS TO THE PACIFIC NORTHWEST. AS YOU FOLLOW THEIR ROUTE, YOU'LL EXPLORE THE WILDERNESS BY KEELBOAT, CANOE, HORSEBACK, AND ON FOOT. ALONG THE WAY, YOU'LL MEET NATIVE AMERICAN TRIBES, SEE SPECTACULAR PLACES, AND ENCOUNTER UNFAMILIAR PLANTS AND ANIMALS. YOUR SURVIVAL DEPENDS ON KNOWLEDGE, SKILL, AND LUCK! FOR GIRLS BETWEEN 7 AND 12, THE AMERICAN GIRL SERIES IS A GREAT LEARNING RESOURCE FOR STUDYING AMERICAN HISTORY, GEOGRAPHY, SOCIAL STUDIES, AND LANGUAGE ARTS, WITHOUT THE "TEXTBOOK" BOREDOM. I USE THESE AS A SPRINGBOARD FOR TEACHING CERTAIN HISTORICAL ERAS. FOR INSTANCE, AFTER READING MEET MOLLY, A BOOK SET IN 1944, WE STUDIED WORLD WAR TWO, THE BOMBING OF PEARL HARBOR, FOOD AND GAS RATIONS, ETC. AFTER READING MEET ADDY, SET IN 1864, WE STUDIED EVERYTHING FROM THE AFRICAN CULTURE TO SLAVERY TO THE ABOLITIONISTS AND THE UNDERGROUND RAILROAD.

APPLE AND STRAWBERRY PICKING WITH FRIENDS.

WORKING PUZZLES AND PLAYING BOARD GAMES WITH SOME INFORMATION OR CHALLENGE. I FOUND THESE HELPED MY YOUNGEST WITH HER DELAYED READING. THESE ACTIVITIES ACTUALLY "GREW" HER BRAIN TO BE ABLE TO TAKE ON DECODING OF WORDS AND PHONICS. AND PARKS ARE ALSO GOOD FOR LEARNING.

1. AGE 9 - EACH BOY RECEIVED A DOUBLE LAUNDRY HAMPER (LIGHTS AND DARKS) AND BEGAN TO DO THEIR OWN LAUNDRY.

2. AGE 10 - OPENED A CHECKING ACCOUNT AND LEARNED TO BALANCE CHECKBOOK.

3. AGE 11 - OPENED A ROTH IRA AND CONTRIBUTED LAWN MOWING EARNINGS. ALSO OPENED A STOCK MARKET ACCOUNT AND BEGAN TO LEARN ABOUT INVESTING.

4. AGE 12 - RECEIVED A BIBLE THAT THEY CAN USE AS AN ADULT IN LEADING THEIR FAMILY IN DEVOTIONS.

5. AGE 13 - RECEIVED A SET OF DEVOTIONAL BOOKS THEY CAN USE WITH THEIR FAMILIES.

6. EVERY YEAR FOR CHRISTMAS/BIRTHDAY, THEY RECEIVE A BOOK THAT MY HUSBAND AND I BELIEVE WILL BE IMPORTANT FOR THEIR FUTURE AND AN ENCOURAGEMENT IN THEIR SPIRITUAL LIFE.

7. THEY HAVE EACH RECEIVED A FILE CABINET AND WE ARE IN THE PROCESS OF HELPING THEM ORGANIZE THEIR FINANCES SO THEY WILL KNOW HOW TO TAKE CARE OF THEIR FAMILIES.

8. THEY EACH HAVE A "MEMORY" NOTEBOOK. THIS CONTAINS THREE SECTIONS (BIBLE, HYMNS, AND OTHER (LIKE POETRY). THEY STORE THE THINGS THEY HAVE MEMORIZED IN THIS BOOK. THEY ARE TO REVIEW IT MONTHLY. I HOPE THIS WILL HELP THEM TO REMEMBER THE THINGS THEY HAVE WORKED ON IN THEIR CHILDHOOD.

9. ANOTHER IDEA IS TO MAKE A "MISSIONS" NOTEBOOK. THIS IS WHERE YOU FILE THE NEWSLETTERS YOU RECEIVE FROM THE DIFFERENT MISSIONARIES YOU SUPPORT. IT IS A GOOD THING TO HELP YOU PRAY.

10. WE ALSO ENJOY ENTERING ESSAY COMPETITIONS INSTEAD OF THE USUAL WRITING ASSIGNMENTS.

REENACTMENT ACTIVITIES GEARED TO A SPECIFIC TIME PERIOD INCLUDING PRIMITIVE CAMPING, COSTUMING, FOOD PREPARATION AND RECIPES, ETC.

I THINK THE #1 "ACTIVITY" WOULD BE VOLUNTEERING - ESPECIALLY IF IT CAN BE DONE AS A FAMILY.

BOY SCOUTS... GREAT WAY FOR YOUR BOYS TO LEARN "PRACTICAL SKILLS" AND LEARN OUTDOOR SKILLS THEY WILL USE THEIR WHOLE LIVES.

WE'VE BEEN DOING IT TOGETHER AS A FAMILY AT A NURSING HOME, AND MY CHILDREN HAVE BEEN DOING IT AT THE LIBRARY. ANOTHER WAY WE VOLUNTEER, IS IF ANYONE IN THE CHURCH (OR WHERE EVER) NEEDS HELP WITH MOVING, THE CHURCH HAS A "WORK DAY" OR SOMEONE NEEDS SOME OTHER KIND OF ASSISTANCE. IT'S SO IMPORTANT FOR OUR CHILDREN TO HAVE A SERVANTS HEART. WHAT BETTER WAY TO INSTILL THAT, THAN FOR THEM TO SEE THEIR PARENTS DEMONSTRATE IT?

ONE THING WE LIKE TO DO IS USE GAMES IN OUR SCHOOL. WE PLAY GAMES THAT MAKE YOU THINK OR PROBLEM SOLVE. SOME EXAMPLES ARE RUMMICUBE, MEMORY, MONOPOLY, GO FISH OR WAR (WITH THE YOUNGER ONES), FRACTION LOTTO, PARTS OF SPEECH BINGO AND CHESS. THERE ARE SO MANY. IT'S A LOT OF FUN AND IT'S NOT TIME WASTED. THERE CAN BE GOOD MEMORIES THERE.

DATE TIME WITH DADDY. IT IS AN ACTUAL TRAINING TIME FOR DADDY TO TEACH THE GIRLS HOW LADIES ARE TO BE TREATED BY YOUNG MEN. ALTHOUGH, OUR GIRLS DON'T KNOW IT. :)

INTEGRATING THE NEEDS TO LEARN INTO OUR DAILY LIFE, LITTLE LESSONS THAT ARE "CAUGHT" AND AMAZINGLY, REMEMBERED SO WELL. WE HAVE ENJOYED DOING LONG-TERM CRAFTS (SEWING), SCIENCE IN ACTION (PRESSURE BOTTLE ROCKETS AND SEED GROWTH), YOU NAME IT, I TRY TO INSERT IT INTO OUR DAILY LIFE, SO THAT IT BECOMES PERSONAL TO OUR KIDS, AND THEY REALLY MAKE IT PART OF THEIR LIVES. THEY'VE REALLY LOVED TO LEARN, AND I THINK THAT'S SETTING US UP FOR MANY MORE LEARNING ADVENTURES.

THIS PAST YEAR WE HAVE RAISED CHICKENS :-) IT'S BEEN A LOT OF FUN. WE GOT OUR CHICKS WHEN THEY WERE ONLY 2 DAYS OLD AND KEPT THEM UNTIL THEY WERE 7 WEEKS. ALL EXPERIENCED THE 'JOY' OF FEEDING AND INTERACTING WITH THE CHICKENS. WE ALSO HAD TO CLEAN THE PEN. THAT WAS NOT SO MUCH FUN! AFTER THE 7 WEEKS, WE WERE ALL ABLE TO ENJOY EATING OUR CHICKENS.

WE PARTICIPATED IN A GEOGRAPHY PROJECT WHICH INVOLVED HOMESCHOOL FAMILIES FROM AROUND THE WORLD. EACH FAMILY MADE QUILT SQUARES. ON THE SQUARE, WE PUT SOMETHING UNIQUE TO OUR PROVINCE. WE EXCHANGED QUILT SQUARES WITH OTHER FAMILIES. WHEN FINISHED, WE WERE ABLE TO MAKE A BEAUTIFUL QUILT.

PERHAPS AT THE TOP OF THE LIST, IS GOING TO THE HOME EDUCATION CONVENTION AND GRADUATION EVERY YEAR. SEEING AND TALKING WITH OTHER LIKE-MINDED PARENTS IS EXTREMELY ENCOURAGING AND ENERGIZING. LIKEWISE, SEEING OTHER HOMESCHOOLED STUDENTS GRADUATE IS AN ENCOURAGEMENT FOR US TO KEEP GOING WITH OUR EYES ON OUR LONG TERM GOALS — RAISING AND EDUCATING OUR CHILDREN SO THEY WILL BECOME THE RESPONSIBLE, EDUCATED ADULTS THEY WERE MEANT TO BE.

Our All-Time favorite activities:

Our favorite family games:

Things that Delight Our Kids
that we need to do more of:

FRUGAL FAMILY FUN TIME IDEAS:

Having fun and making memories with your family doesn't have to cost an arm and a leg. There are all sorts of creative ways for the family to have fun, be together, and spend little if any money. All it takes is a little resourcefulness, creativity, an open mind and a young heart. Read through these ideas, grab one and run with it, or brainstorm your own tweaks and twists to create some treasured family times together. Nothing's better than laughing with your family, and laughs are free.

WE WILL PACK DINNER (OR EVEN BUY A CHEAP ONE - PIZZA, TACOS ETC.) TAKE IT TO A PARK DURING THE WEEK DURING DINNER HOUR. HARDLY ANYONE AROUND SO WE HAVE THE WHOLE PLACE TO OURSELVES. FRISBEE IS GOOD AND ANYTHING YOU CAN THINK OF TO SPEND TIME BEING ACTIVE TOGETHER.

WE PLAY A LOT OF BOARD GAMES. FOR BIRTHDAYS AND CHRISTMAS WE OFTEN GET EVEN MORE...WE HAVE AN ENTIRE CLOSET FULL OF GAMES! WE HAVE PURCHASED THEM FROM RESALE SHOPS, EBAY, AND FRIENDS WHOSE CHILDREN HAVE OUTGROWN GAMES. WE ARE ENJOYING THE FACT THAT BECAUSE OUR CHILDREN ARE BOTH READING THEY CAN PLAY MOST ANY GAMES NOW.

OUR COMMUNITY HAS A WALKING/BIKING TRAIL THAT RUNS ALONGSIDE THE RIVER. IT IS SURPRISINGLY UNDERUSED, MAKING IT A QUIET PLACE TO SPEND TIME TOGETHER OUTDOORS. WE ENJOY PACKING UP BIKES AND JOG STROLLER FOR THE KIDS, THE DOG AND HIS LEASH, LOTS OF WATER FOR EVERYONE AND A CAMERA. IT'S AN INEXPENSIVE WAY TO GET SOME GOOD EXERCISE OUTDOORS TOGETHER. WE ALSO ENJOY CAMPING. THERE ARE SEVERAL LOVELY CAMPGROUNDS WITHIN AN HOUR OF HOME, SO IT DOESN'T COST A LOT IN GAS TO GET THERE. WE FIND THAT EQUIPMENT FOR CAR CAMPING IS MUCH, MUCH LESS EXPENSIVE THAN OUTFITTING FOR BACKPACK TRIPS. ONCE EVERYONE IS SET UP, CAMPING COSTS VERY LITTLE AND BUILDS SOME WONDERFUL FAMILY MEMORIES.

WE LOVE TO GO HIKING IN OUR AREA. THERE ARE MANY LOCAL TRAILS, NATURAL AREAS, AND STATE/COUNTY PARKS. WE PACK UP A PICNIC LUNCH AND GO EXPLORING ON A NATURE WALK, TAKING TIME TO ENJOY THE SCENERY AND ALSO LEARN A LITTLE ABOUT THE LOCAL FLORA AND FAUNA.

HIKING. MOST PLACES HAVE SOMETHING INTERESTING TO GO WALK THROUGH. WE LOVE TO HIKE. MOUNTAINS AND RIVERS ARE FAVORITES, BUT MEADOWS ARE GREAT TOO. EVEN CITIES CAN BE GREAT PLACES TO HIKE. USUALLY THERE WILL BE A PARK, YOU MIGHT MAKE AN OBSTACLE COURSE. OR TRY SCAVENGER HUNTS, OR INFORMATION SEARCHES. YOU MAY THINK YOU KNOW YOUR TOWN OR CITY, BUT YOU WILL BE AMAZED WHAT YOU DON'T KNOW! NOT INTO HIKING? TAKE A BICYCLE RIDE, OR EVEN A CAR RIDE AND LOOK AT WHAT IS AROUND YOU. NO ONE FUSSES (WE HAVE A TWENTY YEAR SPAN IN OUR CHILDREN, SO FINDING ACTIVITIES THAT EVERYONE ENJOYS CAN BE A CHALLENGE, BUT THIS HAS WORKED FOR YEARS!) WE USUALLY TAKE CAMERAS AND THEN THERE IS ANOTHER ACTIVITY WHEN WE GET BACK: PHOTO ALBUMS, TANGIBLE OR ON THE COMPUTER AND REMINISCING.

WE WERE ABLE TO GET A FAMILY MEMBERSHIP TO OUR ZOO FOR $75 FOR THE YEAR. WE COULD THEN GO FOR FREE ALL YEAR. WE ALSO LIKE TO GO TO THE PET STORE AND LOOK AT FISH AND BIRDS AND WHAT EVER ELSE THEY HAVE ON DISPLAY. SOMETIMES WE GRAB DOLLAR BURGERS ON OUR OUTINGS BUT I PREFER HEALTHIER FOODS(: SOMETIMES WE GO MALL WALKING (SUMMER TEXAS HEAT). KINDA GIVES THE KIDS THE IDEA THAT YOU DON'T ALWAYS HAVE TO BUY SOMETHING. AND OF COURSE, THE PARK. WE HAVE A GREAT PARK WITH A TRAIL THAT WRAPS AROUND A LARGE POND.

WE ENJOY A STATE'S PARK PASS IT'S AROUND $50 FOR THE ENTIRE YEAR AND IS GOOD FOR ALL THE STATE PARKS AND MONUMENTS IN THE STATE. IT PAYS FOR ITSELF VERY QUICKLY. WE GET TO ENJOY THE HISTORY AND BEAUTY OF OUR STATE.

CAMPING. IT MIGHT COST A BIT AT FIRST TO BUY A TENT ETC. BUT ONCE THAT'S BOUGHT IT'S REALLY A CHEAP WEEKEND. YOU HAVE TO EAT ANYWAY, SO FOOD'S NOT AN ISSUE. JUST YOUR GAS TO GET WHERE YOU'RE GOING. STATE PARKS AND NATIONAL FOREST CAMPING IS GREAT!

I LOVE TO TAKE MY KIDS TO AREA MUSEUMS - YOU DON'T KNOW AS MUCH ABOUT YOUR AREA AS YOU THINK! PREPARE TO BE SURPRISED!!!

GO TO A STREAM AND SEARCH FOR ANYTHING THAT'S IN THE WATER. JUST TAKE SOME BUCKETS, NETS AND SO WITH YOU AND SEARCH!

GOING TO ANTIQUE STORES AND SEEING THINGS THAT GRANDMA AND GRANDPA GREW UP USING; GOING TO THE FAIR AND SEEING THE SAME THINGS IN THE EXHIBIT HALL. GOING TO MUSEUMS; THERE ARE MANY LOW OR NO-COST MUSEUMS IN SMALL TOWNS, IN OLD COURTHOUSE, OLD JAILS, ETC.

VISITING FARMS FOR LOCAL PRODUCE. WE STAY WITH IN A 50 MILE RADIUS OF HOME. WE LIKE TO DO THIS ON WEEKENDS SO THE WHOLE FAMILY IS ABLE TO GO. IT'S AMAZING THAT WE CAN FIND ALMOST HIDDEN HISTORY MARKERS ON THE ROADS AS WE GO. MAKE IT A GAME TO LOOK FOR THEM. PARK CAREFULLY AND THEN GET OUT AND READ IT! WE BRING A NOTEBOOK TO WRITE DOWN WHERE IT IS AND WHAT IT IS ABOUT. WE KEEP A NOTEBOOK ON OUR STATE HISTORY AND COMPILE BY THE END OF THE SCHOOL YEAR.

WE CHECK OUT THE PASSES AT THE LIBRARY AND VISIT THE MUSEUM OF FINE ARTS, MUSEUM OF SCIENCE, THE PLANETARIUM. WE HAVE FRIENDS WHO LIVE IN NEARBY TOWNS- THEY GET THE PASSES FROM THEIR LIBRARIES AND WE GO AS A GROUP- FUN!

OUR FAVORITE OUTING IS HIKING AND/OR GEOCACHING. GEOCACHING, IN CASE YOU DON'T KNOW WHAT IT IS, IS TAKING A SET OF COORDINATES GIVEN BY SOMEONE ELSE AND FINDING THE LOCATION USING A GPS. USUALLY WHOEVER PLANTED THE CACHE PUT AN AMMO BOX OR TUPPERWARE/RUBBERMAID CONTAINER AT THE CACHE SITE WITH LITTLE TRINKETS AND A LOGBOOK. WHOEVER IS SEARCHING FOR THE CACHE TAKES A TRINKET WITH THEM AND SWAPS IT FOR SOMETHING OUT OF THE CACHE AND THEN LOGS THEIR CACHE NAME WITH DATE AND WHATEVER COMMENTS IN THE LOG BOOK. IT'S A LOT OF FUN AND GREAT EXERCISE.

WE CAMP YEAR-ROUND, WE LOVE TO SWIM AND HIKE AS WELL. NATURE STUDY WOULD HAVE TO BE OUR NUMBER ONE OUTDOOR ACTIVITY AND IT'S OFTEN FREE OTHER THAN THE GAS. WE TALK ABOUT WHAT WE SEE ALONG THE TRAIL OR IN THE WATER, COMPARE WATER QUALITY USING THE PLANTS AND ANIMALS IN AND NEAR THE WATER AS MARKERS (MANY WATER 'BUGS' WILL ONLY LIVE IN EITHER CLEAN OR POLLUTED WATER-NOT BOTH). WE LOOK FOR NESTS, WATCH BIRD FLIGHT PATTERNS, TRY TO ID FLOWERS AND TREES AND INSECTS. WE ALL TAKE LOTS OF PICTURES, MY DAUGHTER LIKES TO DRAW FROM HER SHOTS, THE BOYS USE THEM AS BACKGROUNDS FOR STOP-MOTION ANIMATION.

LOAD UP THE BICYCLES, HEAD TO A GOOD TRAIL AND SPEND THE DAY EXPLORING. MOST CITIES AND AREAS NOW HAVE GREAT BIKE AND WALKING TRAILS. PACK A LIGHT LUNCH AND MAKE A DAY OF IT. BRING ALONG A CAMERA BECAUSE YOU NEVER WHAT YOU WILL SEE AND YOU ARE SURE TO WANT TO CAPTURE SOME OF THE BEAUTY YOU WITNESS TO REMEMBER.

THIS SUMMER WE DID A TOUR OF THE LIBRARIES IN OUR COUNTY. OUR COUNTY HAS 18 LIBRARIES. IT GAVE THE KIDS A CHANCE TO SEE HOW DIFFERENT THE LIBRARIES ARE AND WHERE THE BOOKS THAT THEY REQUEST ONLINE COME FROM! BEST OF ALL – IT WAS FREE!

REMEMBER KIDS OF ALL AGES TRULY JUST CHERISH YOUR TIME AND ATTENTION AND HEARING THE STORY OF THEIR FAMILIES. SOME OF OUR MOST CHERISHED MEMORIES ARE WHEN WE SIT ON OUR BACK PORCH AND JUST LET THE CONVERSATION FLOW NATURALLY. TIME AND ATTENTION ARE STILL THE MOST VALUED POSSESSIONS WE HAVE BUT COULD NEVER AFFORD TO DO WITH OUT. SOCIAL SKILLS ARE ACQUIRED AND A CONNECTION TO LAST A LIFETIME IS FORGED. MORALS ARE PASSED ON. WE LEARN THINGS ABOUT HOW OUR CHILDREN THINK AND THEY LEARN ABOUT US AS PEOPLE NOT JUST PARENTS. TRUE FACE TO FACE CONVERSATION IS SO UNDER-RATED AND YET VERY NECESSARY TO A SUCCESSFUL AND HAPPY LIFE.

TAKE ADVANTAGE OF THE MANY THINGS AVAILABLE IN THE COMMUNITY. A LOT OF CHURCHES HAVE FUN, FREE ACTIVITIES THROUGHOUT THE YEAR (INCLUDING GIVE-AWAYS, FESTIVALS, ETC). THE PARK IS ALWAYS FUN. WHEN WE HAD JUST LITTLE KIDS, WE'D SOMETIMES GO TO MCD AND GET A LARGE FRY AND A DRINK AND LET THE KIDS CLIMB THROUGH THE TUNNELS IN THE WINTER. YOU CAN TAKE WALKS/BIKE RIDES AROUND THE NEIGHBORHOOD. MANY MUSEUMS AND SCIENCE CENTERS HAVE FREE DAYS.

GENERALLY FUN THAT REQUIRES MUCH MONEY ISN'T FOCUSED ON EACH OTHER - IT'S FOCUSED ON THE ITEM YOU ARE SPENDING FUN ON - YOU ARE LOOKING AWAY FROM YOUR FAMILY MEMBER. THEN THERE IS STRESS ON THE PARENT'S PART (SUCH AS AT DISNEY) THEY ARE SPENDING A LOT OF MONEY SO THE FAMILY BETTER ENJOY IT - WHICH DIMINISHES THE FUN. JUST SITTING AROUND THE TABLE AFTER DINNER LAUGHING TOGETHER, TAKING A WALK, OR SITTING AROUND A FIRE IN THE COOL FALL EVENINGS FOCUSES ATTENTION AND LOVE ON YOUR FAMILY MEMBERS NOT ON AN OUTSIDE EVENT. LISTENING TO AUDIO STORIES WHILE WORKING TOGETHER CAN ALSO PROVIDE SOME FUN FAMILY TIMES. THIS IS PART OF THE REASON OUR FAMILY CHOOSES NOT TO OWN VIDEO GAMES, OR HAVE TV IN OUR HOME. FOCUS ON EACH OTHER - THERE ARE MANY FREE EVENTS IN THE AREA THAT DO THAT. OCCASIONALLY IT IS NICE TO DO SOMETHING OUTSIDE THAT REALM - SO CHOOSE TO GO TO A MUSEUM - WHERE YOU LEARN TOGETHER AND THEN YOU HAVE SOMETHING TO DISCUSS AND REMEMBER AS YOU SIT AROUND THAT FIRE AGAIN! :)

TALK TO LOCAL FAMILIES ABOUT LOCAL OPPORTUNITIES. WE DIDN'T KNOW FOR 3 YEARS THAT WE LIVED 15 MINUTES FROM A STATE PARK THAT HAD A LAKESIDE "BEACH" AREA FOR PUBLIC SWIMMING (COST IS $5 PER VEHICLE)! TALK TO YOUR LOCAL LIBRARIANS, TOO, ESPECIALLY IN THE CHILDREN'S DEPARTMENT-- THEY MAKE IT THEIR BUSINESS TO KNOW ALL ABOUT KIDS ACTIVITIES IN THE AREA. (ALSO, IF THE LIBRARIANS KNOW YOU THEY MIGHT EVEN "SQUEEZE YOU IN" FOR A LIBRARY EVENT THAT'S ALREADY FULL TO CAPACITY!)

STEER CLEAR OF TOURIST ATTRACTIONS AND MAINSTREAM ENTERTAINMENT. FOCUS ON BUILDING RELATIONSHIPS RATHER THAN BEING ENTERTAINED. SERVICE PROJECTS AND VOLUNTEERING ARE THE VERY BEST KIND OF FAMILY FUN WE CAN HAVE!

MY GIRLS AND I ENJOY GOING TO GARAGE SALES. THEY HAVE LEARNED HOW TO BARGAIN FOR BETTER DEALS AND LOVE GOING TO FIND A GOOD DEAL!

DO AWAY WITH WHAT OUR CULTURE SAYS FUN MUST BE. ENTERTAINMENT DOES NOT EQUAL FUN. MOVIES, TELEVISION... ETC.... THESE ARE NOT FUN. THEY DO NOT ALLOW FOR FAMILY INTERACTION. YOU SIT IN SILENCE BESIDE EACH OTHER. THROW OUT YOUR TV!! OR JUST KEEP IT FOR SPECIAL DAYS. DO EVERYTHING TOGETHER - WORK TOGETHER, PLAY TOGETHER. GO TO AUCTIONS, VISIT LOCAL FARMS, JOIN 4H, VISIT LOCAL HISTORICAL SITES AND GET TO KNOW THE HISTORY OF YOUR REGION. PLANT A GARDEN. SERVE YOUR LOCAL CHURCH TOGETHER - IF YOU HAVE A FELLOWSHIP TIME, VOLUNTEER AS A FAMILY TO SERVE THE REFRESHMENTS.

LOTS OF PLACES HAVE HOMESCHOOL DAYS, WHEN HOMESCHOOL FAMILIES CAN GET IN FOR FREE; CUSTOMER APPRECIATION DAYS W/ FREE ADMISSION OR FREE ACTIVITIES, FOOD, ETC.; LOCAL FESTIVALS ARE OFTEN FREE IF YOU PLAN TO FOREGO THE EXPENSIVE FESTIVAL FOODS AND SOUVENIRS.

FOR THE YOUNGER KIDS, CRAYON HIKES ARE EASY AND OFTEN FREE-IT DOES NOT MATTER WHAT CONDITION THE CRAYON IS IN. WALK AROUND WITH A BOX OF CRAYONS OUTSIDE IN THE SAME AREA ONCE A MONTH AND SEE HOW MANY COLORS YOU CAN MATCH WITH NATURE AND MANMADE ITEMS. LOOKING AT THE STARS, DANCING TO MUSIC, HAVING A FAMILY BOOK CLUB AND EVERYONE READ THE SAME BOOK, DISCUSS, THEN WATCH THE MOVIE BASED ON THE BOOK-THERE ARE HUNDREDS OF CHOICES.

ONE OF THE BEST THINGS WE HAVE FOUND ABOUT BEING HOMESCHOOLERS IS WE CAN VACATION WHEN THE REST OF THE KIDS ARE IN SCHOOL. WE TAKE VACATIONS ON THE SHOULDER SEASON WHEN EVERYTHING IS HALF PRICE AND THERE ARE NO LINES. WE WERE ACTUALLY ABLE TO RENT A COTTAGE FOR A WHOLE WEEK FOR $300 IN A VERY POPULAR BEACH RESORT AREA SIMPLY BECAUSE IT WAS THE WEEK BEFORE HIGH SEASON. OF COURSE WITH A FULLY SERVICED COTTAGE, YOU CAN PREPARE ALL YOUR MEALS RIGHT THERE SO NO EATING OUT EXPENSE. THE BEACH AND PARKS ARE YOURS TO EXPLORE WITHOUT THE HEAVY TRAFFIC.

WE TAKE ADVANTAGE OF THE SMALL TOWN FAIRS AND CELEBRATIONS AROUND THE AREA. WE USUALLY BRING OUR OWN FOOD BUT WILL TRY ONE SPECIALITY ITEM AT THE EVENT. WE ALSO GO TO THE ICE CREAM SHOP AND THEN SIT BY THE WATER AND WATCH THE BOATS.

SOMETHING MY FIL STARTED WAS PUTTING BUBBLES IN THE KIDDIE POOL OUTSIDE. FUN AND BATH TIME ALL IN ONE(: HE USES A SPRAYER NOZZLE TO GET IT REALLY BUBBLY. WE ALSO LIKE TO CREATE "ABSTRACTS". WE ALL GET A SHEET OF PRINTER PAPER AND FILL THE PAGE WITH DIFFERENT COLORS, SHAPES OR WHAT EVER, THE IDEA IS TO COMPLETELY FILL THE PAGE. THEN WE SEE HOW DIFFERENT EVERYONES TURNS OUT. WE'LL USE CRAYONS, MARKERS, COLORED PENCILS, PASTELS OR ANY COMBINATION. IT CAN TAKE UP TO AN HOUR TO FINISH ONE BUT WE'VE TURNED OUT SOME REALLY COOL LOOKING "ART". CAMPING CAN BE PRETTY FRUGAL AND AN ABSOLUTELY AMAZING FAMILY TIME(: SOMETIMES WE WILL JUST SET UP THE TENT IN THE PLAY ROOM AND READ STORIES AND LET THE KIDS CAMP OUT IN THERE. WE HAVE 4 KIDS AND THEY ALL SLEEP IN ONE ROOM AND ALL THEIR TOYS ARE IN 3RD BEDROOM SO THEY ARE USED TO SLEEPING ALL TOGETHER.

TRADITIONS, TRADITIONS, TRADITIONS....HAVE A FAMILY GAME NIGHT, HAVE A MAKE PIZZA NIGHT. I HAVE FOUND IT IS THE MONEY OR THE GLAMOUROUS THINGS...MY KIDS LOVE AND THRIVE ON OUR SIMPLEST OF TRADITIONS...SATURDAY PANCAKE BREAKFASTS MADE AT HOME....JUST SPEND TIME TOGETHER!

COOKING A MEAL TOGETHER IS FUN. GIVING EACH PERSON A PART TO PREPARE. ANOTHER THING THAT COMES TO MIND IS WORK AROUND THE HOUSE. I KNOW IT'S NOT "FUN" BUT WHEN WE DO IT ALL TOGETHER, SOMEHOW WE END UP HAVING FUN.

USE RECYCLABLE MATERIALS TO MAKE FOUND ART WITH YOUR KIDS. CHECK OUT MOVIES OR BOOKS ON TAPE FROM THE LOCAL LIBRARY AND HAVE A FAMILY NIGHT INCLUDING GAMES. HAVE A FUN READ-ALOUD NIGHT AND TAKE TURNS READING PASSAGES FROM FAVORITE BOOKS.

DO ART PROJECTS. WHEN THE KIDS WERE YOUNGER SHAVING CREAM ON A TABLE LASTED FOR HOURS OF FUN, MAKING PLAYDOUGH. NOW THAT THEY ARE OLDER 12 AND 15 I FOUND THIS WEEK THEY STILL LIKE MAKING COLLAGES. WE HAD OLD MAGAZINES AND I CHALLENGED THEM TO FILL THE WHITE SPACE WITH SHAPES (PUNCHES I HAD), OR CREATE LINES/PATTERNS WITH COLOR. THE RESULTS ARE BEAUTIFUL AND PRACTICALLY FREE

WE ALSO GET A LOT OF LAUGHS HAVING WATER GUN AND WATER HOSE FIGHTS IN OUR COURTYARD (WE LIVE IN PUERTO RICO). THE DOG JOINS IN AS WE SPRAY EACH OTHER UNTIL WE ARE DRENCHED. THEN IT'S TIME FOR SHOWERS AND DINNER. IT IS A GREAT WAY TO COOL OFF AND GET SOME PHYSICAL ACTIVITY THAT INCLUDES THE WHOLE FAMILY.

MAKE UP YOUR OWN GAMES, CHANGE THE RULES TO GAMES YOU ALREADY KNOW, OR COMBINE GAMES TO MAKE A NEW GAME TO PLAY. GET CREATIVE AND MAKE COSTUMES OUT OF THINGS AROUND THE HOUSE AND MAKE UP A SKIT TO ACT OUT. SEE WHAT KINDS OF THINGS YOU CAN COME UP WITH TO RECYCLE AND MAKE NEW AGAIN TO USE AS DECORATIONS OR GIFTS FOR OTHERS.

WE HAVE A "COMPETITION" TO SEE IF WE CAN FEED OUR FAMILY (OF 7, SOMETIMES 9 IF THE GRANDKIDS ARE HERE) FOR UNDER $10. I'VE GOTTEN REALLY GOOD AT IT AND A LOT OF TIMES THOSE MEALS ARE THE BEST. IT HELPS THE KIDS IN MATH AND IT'S FUN WHEN WE CAN ANNOUNCE THE AMOUNT SPENT ON THE MEAL.

ANYTIME WE COOK SOMETHING TOGETHER, JUST FOR FUN...IS A GREAT TIME! WE LOVE TO COOK OUTDOORS...WE GET THE FOLDING TABLES OUT AND MAKE THINGS LIKE APPLE PIE, BREAD OR PIZZA! WITH LOTS OF KIDS THE MESS STAYS OUTSIDE AND MOM/DAD BRING IT INSIDE TO COOK IT!

I THINK THE DIGITAL CAMERA SCAVENGER HUNTS ARE FUN. YOU GET A LIST OF THINGS TO FIND, TAKE YOUR DIGITAL CAMERAS IN HAND, AND GO TAKE PICS. IN THE CASE OF A TIE, BEST PIC WINS.

ONE OF THE FUNNEST THINGS WE DID THIS SUMMER WAS
SAVE CEREAL BOXES AND WE ENLISTED THE HELP OF OUR FRIENDS.
WE SAVED ALL FOOD BOXES AND LARGER BOXES TOO.
THEN WE HAD A PLAYDATE AND BUILT A HUGE CEREAL BOX HOUSE
IN THE PLAYROOM WITH ALL OUR FRIENDS!

SCRAPBOOKING IS A FAVORITE OF OURS. WHAT WE DO IS RECYCLE GRAPHICS AND WORD ART FROM MAGAZINES, GREETING CARDS, JUNK MAIL, ETC. WE ALSO USE FREE SCRAPBOOKING PRINTABLES AND CLIP ART. EACH OF MY CHILDREN USE THIS PROCESS TO MAKE THEIR OWN HOMESCHOOL YEARBOOKS. IT'S A GREAT WAY FOR THE KIDS TO STORE SCHOOL ITEMS THAT ARE SPECIAL TO THEM, BUT NOT NECESSARY FOR PORTFOLIO'S. AND THE ONLY COST I HAVE IS COPIES OF DIGITAL PHOTOS, PRINTER PAPER, AND SHEET PROTECTORS. WE USE OLD BINDER DIVIDERS FOR COLORED CARDSTOCK :)

BONFIRE IN THE BACKYARD!
WE ALWAYS FEEL LIKE WE'RE CAMPING AND LOVE TO
ROAST MARSHMALLOWS...BUT WHEN YOU'RE DONE YOU GET TO SLEEP IN YOUR
OWN BED! THIS WORKS EVEN IN THE BBQ W/ THE WARM COALS.

WE LIKE TO PLAY LAWN BOWLING. YOU PUT OUT A TARGET BALL AND EVERYONE GETS FOUR BALLS TO THROW- THE OBJECT IS TO BE THE PERSON WHO GETS ONE OF THEIR BALLS CLOSEST TO THE TARGET BALL.

AT NIGHT WE PLAY FIREFLY TAG...EVERYONE HAS A FLASHLIGHT AND ALL
EXCEPT THE PERSON WHO IS 'IT' HIDE. THOSE WHO ARE HIDING MUST HOLD
THE FLASHLIGHT IN FRONT OF THEIR CHIN AND COUNT TO 10 (ONE, MISSISSIPPI,
TWO, MISSISSIPPI, ETC.) AND TURN ON THEIR FLASHLIGHT ONLY FOR THE COUNT OF 10.
EACH NEEDS TO RUN TO A HOME BASE, WHOEVER IS CAUGHT FIRST IS 'IT'.
THE PERSON WHO IS 'IT' ALSO HAS A FLASHLIGHT THAT CAN BE USED TO SEEK OUT
THE REST OF THE PLAYERS.

WE LIKE TO USE ALL THE PILLOWS, CHAIRS, BLANKETS, ETC TO MAKE A GIANT FORT OUT OF OUR LIVING ROOM. THE KIDS CAN PLAY IN THERE FOR HOURS AND IT'S EVEN FUN FOR THEM TO "INVITE" MOM AND DAD TO "THEIR HOUSE" FOR LUNCH :)

I LIKE TO SHOP THE THRIFT STORES FOR BOARD GAMES. I HAVE FOUND SOME REALLY UNIQUE OLDER GAMES THAT JUST AREN'T MADE ANYMORE. WE LIKE TO PLAY TOGETHER IN THE EVENINGS.

PLAYING A GAME CALLED "WHO, WHAT, WHEN, WHERE, WHY. WE LEARNED IT ON ZOOM. EACH PERSON HAS PAPER AND PENCIL. EVERYONE WRITES "WHO" THEN THEY WRITE WHO THEIR WHO IS. (PERSON, ALIEN, DINOSAUR ETC.) WITHOUT LETTING ANYONE SEE THEIR ANSWER. THEN EVERYONE FOLDS OVER THEIR ANSWER AND PASSES IT TO THE PERSON BESIDE THEM. NOW, EVERYONE WRITES "WHAT" AND THEN WRITES THEIR "WHAT" (EXAMPLE: PREPARES FOOD FOR A PICNIC). REMEMBER NOT TO SHOW ANYONE THEN FOLD OVER THEIR ANSWER AND PASS TO THE NEXT PERSON. CONTINUE THIS WITH "WHEN", "WHERE" AND "WHY". THEN WHEN EVERYONE HAS FINISHED THEIR "WHY" ANSWER, EACH PERSON UNFOLDS THE PAPER THAT THEY HAVE LAST AND TAKE TURNS READING THE STORY THAT HAS BEEN CREATED ON THEIR PAGE. HILARIOUS!

WE DO WHAT WE CALL FORT NIGHT. WE TAKE OLD SHEETS AND MAKE A FORT OUT OF THEM IN THE LIVING ROOM. WE MAKE SURE THE TV IS INSIDE THE FORT. WE GET FREE MOVIES FROM THE LIBRARY, POP OUR OWN POPCORN, BRING OUR SLEEPING BAGS INSIDE THE FORT, AND WATCH A MOVIE TOGETHER. THEN AFTER THE MOVIES ARE OVER, WE SLEEP IN THE FORT.

TREASURE HUNTS ARE A FAVORITE. THE OLDER KIDS HELP PUT THEM
TOGETHER. WE USE MATH PUZZLES, PICTURE CLUES FOR THE
YOUNGER, RHYMES, RIDDLES, WRITING IN WHITE CRAYON AS A
'SECRET CODE' - YOU HAVE TO COLOR WITH A MARKER TO SEE THE
WRITTEN CLUE. THERE IS USUALLY A 'TREASURE BOX' AT THE END
WITH A TREAT FOR EACH CHILD IN IT. IF YOU HAVE A COUPLE
OLDER KIDS, THEY'LL LOVE MAKING A BUNCH OF TREASURE HUNTS.
I'VE HAD MY KIDS DO FOUR OR FIVE HUNTS AND STAY BUSY AND
HAPPY FOR HOURS.

WE LIKE TO TURN COOKING DINNER INTO OUR OWN COOKING
SHOW. MY HUSBAND OFTEN VIDEO TAPES US AND MY SON LEARNS
A LOT ABOUT COOKING WHILE HE LEARNS TO EXPRESS HIMSELF
(PUBLIC SPEAKING PRACTICE) AS HE EXPLAINS THE STEPS OF THE
RECIPE.

DANCE! WE LOVE TO TURN THE MUSIC UP AND JUST DANCE OR PLAY FREEZE DANCE!
COST: $0

EVERYONE GETS A PAPER (OR 2 OR 3) AND PEN AND STARTS WRITING
FUN THINGS DOWN FOR SOMEONE ELSE, NOT KNOWING WHO WILL GET
THIS PAPER. YOU GET TEN MINUTES (OR 15 OR 20) TO WRITE AND PREPARE.
AFTER THAT WE ALL GET A PAPER FROM SOMEONE ELSE WITH SOMETHING
NICE ON IT LIKE 'LOOK IN THE FRIDGE, I MADE YOU SOMETHING NICE'
OR 'I WILL CHANGE YOUR SHEETS RIGHT NOW' OR 'I WILL MAKE YOUR HAIR
BEAUTIFUL TODAY' (ALWAYS FUNNY WHEN DAD GETS THIS CARD INSTEAD
OF ONE OF THE GIRLS). A FUN AND NICE FAMILY TIME!

WE LOVE TO SNUGGLE UP TOGETHER ON THE SOFA AND READ
CHARACTER BUILDING BOOKS (LAMPLIGHTER BOOKS, ELSIE DINSMORE SERIES,
PILGRIM'S PROGRESS, TIGER AND TOM, KING'S DAUGHTER, CHOICE STORIES
FOR CHILDREN, ETC.)

MY KIDS LOVE TO CAMPOUT IN THE BACKYARD. ONCE WE LET THEM WATCH A MOVIE BY
PROJECTING IT ONTO THE SIDE OF THE HOUSE. THEY ATE POPCORN AND WATCHED THE
MOVIE SNUGGLED IN THEIR SLEEPING BAGS AND BLANKIES.

INVITING FRIENDS OVER TO VISIT. WE LOVE ENTERTAINING FAMILIES OF FRIENDS.
THE PREPARATIONS, LIKE MAKING SPECIAL DISHES, TIDYING AND PREPARING
ACTIVITIES, CAN BE ALMOST AS MUCH FUN AS THE TIME WITH THE GUESTS AS WE
ENJOY CREATIVE TIME TOGETHER.

WE HAVE FRIDAY FAMILY FUN NIGHT. SOMETIMES WE PULL OUT ALL THE THOMAS
TRAINS OR FISHER PRICE DOLL HOUSE AND SET UP EVERYTHING IN THE LIVING ROOM.
EVERYONE PLAYS. DADDY, MOMMY, OLDER KIDS AND YOUNGER. WE ALSO GET
DADDY'S OLD GIANT ARCHITECTURE PAPER, TAPE IT TO THE FLOOR, AND HAVE DRAWING
CONTESTS.

WE ABSOLUTELY LOVE MAKING VIDEOS ON OUR CAMERA AND THEN PLAY THEM ON THE
TV. WE USE THE WII, WHICH IS EXTRA FUN, TO PLAY THEM BACKWARDS TOO. WE LAUGH
SOOO HARD!

WE PLAY 20 QUESTIONS. THE TOPIC CAN BE ANYTHING FROM BIBLE, TO GEOGRAPHY, TO MATH, TO CURRENT EVENTS, TO HISTORY...ETC. (YOU GET THE IDEA). ONE PERSON IS "IT." THE PERSON WHO IS IT GOES FIRST BY THINKING OF A PERSON, PLACE, OR THING RELATED TO THE TOPIC. FOR EXAMPLE, "I'M THINKING OF SOMEONE FROM THE BIBLE" WOULD BE A GOOD START. THE PEOPLE PLAYING TAKE TURNS GOING AROUND THE ROOM ASKING ONE QUESTION FOR EACH TURN. QUESTIONS SHOULD HELP DISCOVER THE ANSWER. QUESTIONS MUST BE PHRASED AS YES OR NO QUESTIONS. WHEN YOU THINK YOU KNOW THE ANSWER, YOU MUST WAIT YOUR TURN TO GUESS, PHRASING YOUR GUESS AS A YES OR NO QUESTION. SUCH AS "IS THE PERSON YOU ARE THINKING OF FROM THE BIBLE, MOSES?" TURN TAKING CONTINUES UNTIL SOMEONE CORRECTLY GUESSES. THEN THE ONE WHO GUESSED CORRECTLY, GETS TO TAKE HIS OR HER TURN BEING "IT".

FIND SOME FAMILY VIDEOS OR EDUCATIONAL VIDEOS ON THE WEB AND WATCH THEM TOGETHER.

LEARN A NEW CRAFT FROM YOUTUBE, A WEBSITE, OR THE LIBRARY AND DO YOUR CRAFT AT HOME. ORIGAMI CAN BE DONE FOR FREE USING JUNK MAIL PAPER AND FREE FOLDING RESOURCES.

WE LIKE TO SEARCH FOR INTERESTING ROCKS. WHEN WE BRING THEM HOME WE PAINT THEM ALL SORTS OF PRETTY COLORS AND PATTERNS. MY KIDS COULD PAINT ROCKS ALL DAY LONG.

MAKING MOVIES. OUR OLDEST SON IS INTERESTED IN FILM MAKING AND
ALL THE CHILDREN HAVE HAD A TON OF FUN MAKING MOVIES AND EDITING THEM.
THE MOST FUN THEY HAD WAS WHEN THEY FILMED A CHASE SCENE AT A PARK
AND HAD EVERYONE THERE WONDERING WHAT THEY WERE DOING.

WE ARE ALSO A GAME FAMILY SO WE ENJOY A VARIETY OF BOARD GAMES. WE ALSO
WATCH OLD TV SHOW ONLINE AND MOVIES ONLINE SO WE DON'T HAVE TO PAY
THEATER PRICES. WE ALSO LOVE HOSPITALITY SO HAVING PEOPLE TO OUR HOME FOR
TEA PARTIES OR JUST A SIMPLE SNACK AND FELLOWSHIP IS A LOT OF FUN FOR US.
WE PUT ON A GAME NIGHT AT OUR HOME AND INVITED OUR CHURCH (WE ARE IN A
SMALL CHURCH). IT BECAME A FAVORITE TIME OF THE MONTH FOR MANY IN OUR
CHURCH. SO WE HAD FUN AND MINISTERED TO OTHERS AS WELL.

PLAY SQUIGGLE... IT'S AN ACTUAL GAME, BUT ALL YOU HAVE TO DO IS DRAW
THE SAME SQUIGGLE LINE ON EVERYONE'S PIECE OF PAPER AND EVERYONE
GETS 60 SECONDS TO TURN IT INTO SOMETHING RECOGNIZABLE. EVERYONE
USUALLY DRAWS SOMETHING UNIQUE.

WE LOVE PLAYING DODGE BALL IN OUR BACKYARD. WE GET THE SOFTEST BALLS AND
DIVIDE THE TEAM. BY DOING THIS, THE NEIGHBORHOOD KIDS HAVE BEGUN TO DRAW TO
OUR BACKYARD EACH TIME THEY HEAR US. WHEN THEY DON'T WANT TO PLAY DODGE
BALL WE SET UP THE SOCCER NETS OR CORN HOLE.

FOR A DAY THAT HAS BEEN PARTICULARLY STRESSFUL, WE REALLY ENJOY HAVING A GOOD OLD FASHIONED PILLOW FIGHT! IT DOESN'T TAKE MUCH TIME, AND EVEN THE LITTLEST KIDDOS TRY TO FLOP A PILLOW AT DADDY!

ANY OF THE 101 THINGS THAT A CARDBOARD BOX CAN BECOME.
RIGHT NOW, MY KIDS HAVE A 2 STORY CARDBOARD BOX CONDO WITH WINDOWS, DOORS, MAILBOXES, A GARDEN, AND YOU NAME IT! THEY KNOW THEY CAN KEEP THE BOXES UNTIL THEY ARE WORN OUT. GIVE THEM SOME BOXES OF ANY SIZE AND JUST WATCH WHAT THEY BECOME!

WE LIKE TO TAKE TURNS HAVING ONE OF THE KIDS PICK THE RECIPE AND HELP MAKE IT. ANOTHER THING WE DO IS TO LOOK UP SOME RECIPES FROM AROUND THE WORLD AND DO AN INTERNATIONAL MEAL AND TALK ABOUT THAT COUNTRY ONCE A MONTH.

ICE CREAM SUNDAE PARTIES. I LIKE TO PURCHASE ICE CREAM ON SALE AT OUR LOCAL KROGER, GRAB A FEW TOPPINGS AND, VOILA, INSTANT PARTY!

WHEN WE DO HOLIDAY ACTIVITIES, WE HAVE AN OLD FAMILY TRADITION THAT GOES BACK TO AT LEAST MY GREAT-GRANDPARENTS. WE SET UP A COFFEE TABLE AND PUT TOGETHER A JIGSAW PUZZLE. SOMETIMES WE'LL DO A FAMILY GAME NIGHT DURING THE REST OF THE YEAR. WE HAVE GREAT EVENINGS TOGETHER THIS WAY.

WE HAVE A BIG BACK YARD IN WHICH TO COLLECT BUGS, CATERPILLARS, TADPOLES ETC WE MAKE HABITATS AND WATCH THEM. WE HAVE MADE TEEPEES WITH PINE BOUGHS AND IGLOOS IN THE WINTER. RIGHT NOW WE HAVE BEEN EXPERIMENTING WITH STICKS AND FEATHER FOR ARROWS (STUDYING NATIVE AMERICANS) BUT YOU CAN ALSO USE STRAWS AND PAPER. JUST MAKE A SMALL SLIT IN THE STRAW END AND INSERT THE PAPER. HOW DOES IT GO WITHOUT/WITH PAPER? ONE PIECE, MORE? DISTANCE AND ACCURACY

WE HAVE 5 CHILDREN, THE OLDEST IS 7 AND THE GAME THEY ALL LOVE TO PLAY IS HIDE AND SEEK AND REVERSE HIDE AND SEEK. HIDE AND SEEK: TRADITIONAL WHERE EVERYONE HIDES AND 1 PERSON SEEKS. OR REVERSE HIDE AND SEEK WHERE ONE PERSON HIDES AND THEN EVERYONE GOES AND FINDS THEM AND HIDES WITH THEM UNTIL EVERYONE IS TOGETHER. EXAMPLE: 1 PERSON HIDES IN CLOSET THEN 5 OTHERS HAVE TO FIND THE PERSON, SO ONE BY ONE THEN FIND AND HIDE WITH UNTIL THE CLOSET IS FULL OF 5 PEOPLE HIDING TOGETHER--USUALLY FOLLOWED BY LOTS OF GIGGLING!

THEY ALSO LIKE TO PLAY "DON'T EAT____" WE MAKE 9 SQUARES ON A PAPER, 3 DOWN AND 3 ACROSS AND FILL IT WITH PICTURES OF THEIR FAVORITE THINGS. THEN PUT A CANDY, RAISIN, MARSHMALLOW ON EACH SQUARE, ONE PERSON LEAVES AND THE OTHERS PICK A SQUARE. THEN THE PERSON COMES BACK AND STARTS EATING THE TREAT ON EACH SQUARE, UNTIL THEY GET TO THE SQUARE PREVIOUSLY PICKED AND EVERYONE YELLS OUT, "DON'T EAT ___" WE HAVE DONE OPTIMUS PRIME, REMY, EVEN FARM ANIMALS. THE KIDS ARE ALL QUIET UNTIL WE ALL YELL OUT "DON'T EAT..." AND EVERYONE LAUGHS.

ALL OUR KIDS EVER WANT IS OUR UNDIVIDED ATTENTION. SO WE ALWAYS MAKE A POINT TO PUT ALL THE PHONES IN A DRAWER, TURN OFF THE DEVICES, AND HAVE OLD FASHIONED FACE TIME ACTIVITIES WITH THEM. WHETHER IT'S PLAYING BOARD GAMES OR PLAYING BALL OUTSIDE IT DOESN'T REALLY MATTER!

MY CHILDREN LOVE TREASURE HUNTS. I WILL HIDE SOMETHING AND THEN GIVE THEM CLUE #1, THEY DECODE THE CLUE AND FIND ANOTHER CLUE WAITING FOR THEM. SOME TIMES IT IS AS SIMPLE AS HAVING A SPECIAL LUNCH WAITING FOR THEM. OTHER TIMES THERE MIGHT BE A SPECIAL BOOK EACH CHILD HAS BEEN WAITING FOR. THE "TREASURE" IS ONLY A FRACTION OF THE FUN....THE HUNT IS THE OTHER PART! I HAVE BEEN KNOW TO ASK THE NEIGHBORS IF I CAN HIDE CLUES ON THEIR PROPERTY AND IT KEEPS THINGS INTERESTING FOR MY OLDER CHILDREN!

A GAME CALLED HOOPS. IT'S HISTORY IS FROM THE 1800S I BELIEVE. WE MADE OUR OWN WITH EMBROIDIERY HOOPS. TAKE THE BIGGER PIECE AND WRAP RIBBON AROUND IT THEN ABOUT A 1 1/2 DOWEL CUT IN HALF YOU GO OUTSIDE OR IN THE LIVING ROOM AT YOUR OWN RISK AND YOU HAVE TO CATCH THE HOOP ON BOTH DOWELS UP TO 10 POINTS. IT IS FUN YOU CAN LOOK IT UP ON THE INTERNET FOR MORE DETAILS.

WE MAKE UP STORIES TOGETHER. WHEN MOM AND DAD START, IT'S USUALLY BECAUSE ONE OF US HEARS SOMETHING THAT SOUNDS LIKE AN ABSURDITY OR SAID SOMETHING A LITTLE "OFF" OR BACKWARD. SO WE BEGIN A TALL TALE BUILDING ON THAT MISPOKEN OR MISHEARD THING. WHAT IF THERE WERE SUCH A PLACE OR THING? NOW THAT OUR PRESCHOOLER IS BEGINNING TO TELL STORIES OF HER OWN, WE ENCOURAGE HER TO EXPAND. WHEN WE BEGIN WITHOUT HER WITH OUR OWN STORIES, WE ENCOURAGE HER TO JOIN IN WITH VERBS, NAMES, ACTING OUT THE STORY, ETC.

WE TAKE TURNS GIVING "NEWS" REPORTS.....THE OLDER KIDS AND PARENTS ARE THE REPORTERS AND THE YOUNGEST (AGE 4) HAS THE COMMAND. THE 4-YEAR OLD SITS ON A BAR STOOL WITH HIS "MICROPHONE" AND INTRODUCES EACH REPORTER. THE KIDS REPORT ON SOMETHING THEY HAVE LEARNED, 3-4 INTERESTING FACTS. MOM REPORTS ON ANYTHING RECENTLY STUDIED WITH THE KIDS.....OR SOMETHING NEW WITH DRAMATIC FLARE. DAD REPORTS ABOUT SOMETHING IN THE NEWS / WORLD BECAUSE HE'S BEEN LISTING TO CONSERVATIVE TALK RADIO ALL DAY AND HAS GREAT THOUGHTS TO SHARE.

WE ENJOY A GAME WE CALL "FAMILY STORY". ONE PERSON GIVES A TITLE, THEN STARTS TELLING A STORY. AFTER 2-3 SENTENCES, THEY STOP (USUALLY IN THE MIDDLE OF A SENTENCE) AND THE NEXT PERSON TAKES OVER WHERE THEY LEFT OFF. WE CONTINUE UNTIL EACH PERSON HAS HAD A TURN, AND THE LAST PERSON GETS TO TELL THE ENDING. THIS HAS BEEN ESPECIALLY FUN WITH YOUNGER CHILDREN, AS THEY COME UP WITH SOME OF THE WACKIEST AND FUNNIEST PARTS OF THE STORY.

WE LIKE TO TIE-DYE. YOU CAN GET A COUPLE PACKAGES OF RIT DYE FOR FAIRLY CHEAP. SOMETIMES WE BUY INEXPENSIVE T-SHIRTS FROM THE STORE, BUT OTHER TIMES WE TIE-DYE SHIRTS THAT WE ALREADY HAVE. IF A FAVORITE SHIRT GETS A SMALL STAIN, WE DON'T TOSS IT, WE DYE IT. COVERS UP THE STAIN, AND WE HAVE FUN TOGETHER DOING IT.

A FUN AND (MOSTLY) FREE WAY TO EXPERIENCE SCIENCE IS TO GATHER AS MANY 1 OR 2 LITER BOTTLES AS YOU CAN FIND AND GOOGLE "LITER BOTTLE + EXPERIMENT" AND YOU'LL BE MAKING STUFF LIKE CLOUD FORMATIONS, MENTOS EXPLOSIONS, DANCING RAISINS, LIQUID FIREWORKS AND MANY MORE!

WE LOVE HAVING A PICNIC AT HOME ... PREPARE OUR FAVORITE FINGER FOODS, SPREAD OUT A BLANKET TO SIT ON, AND ENJOY A PICNIC WITHOUT THE BUGS! I FIND IT'S NOT REALLY ABOUT THE PICNICKY FOODS, BUT THE FACT THAT "MOM AND DAD ARE SITTING ON THE FLOOR WITH US" THAT THE KIDS ENJOY. WE MOVE AROUND THE HOUSE, TOO ... SOMETIMES WE SIT IN THE LIVING ROOM AROUND THE COFFEE TABLE AND PLAY A CARD OR BOARD GAME, SOMETIMES IN FRONT OF THE TV WHERE WE POP IN A FAMILY-FRIENDLY MOVIE.

BUILDING CAMP SITES WITH ROPE, SHEETS ETC OR EVEN BRANCHES AND FRONDS ETC.
WE HELP BUILD HUTS FOR EACH OTHER UNTIL WE HAVE A LITTLE VILLAGE,
WE USE FOUND OBJECTS AS CURRENCY, TRADE GOODS AND SERVICES,
AND AT THE END OF THE DAY BUILD A CAMP FIRE AND HAVE DINNER AROUND IT.
IF WEATHER ALLOWS WE WILL SLEEP OUTSIDE ALSO -- PURE MAGIC !

WE LIKE TO COOK TOGETHER. BUY FLAT BREAD OR HOAGIE BUNS 2 CUT IN HALF,
PIZZA SAUCE, SHREDDED MOZZARELLA CHEESE, PEPPERONI, VEGGIES OF CHOICE,
AND LET THE KIDS ASSEMBLE THEIR OWN PIZZAS AND BAKE. YOU CAN MAKE COOKIES, BANANA SPITS, OR FRUIT SALAD TOGETHER FOR DESSERT. COOKING TOGETHER IS SO MUCH FUN FOR THE KIDS. NOW, GETTING THEM TO HELP WITH THE CLEAN UP IS ANOTHER MATTER! LOL

WE MAKE OUR OWN "CONSTELLATIONS" BY DRAWING A DESIGN ON BLACK CONSTRUCTION PAPER W/ A WHITE CRAYON, THEN POKING HOLES EVERY SO OFTEN ON THE LINES. WHEN YOU'RE DONE, TURN OFF THE LIGHTS AND HOLD A FLASHLIGHT UNDER THE CONSTRUCTION PAPER, AND YOUR CONSTELLATION WILL SHOW UP ON THE CEILING. IF YOU MAKE SOMETHING SPECIFIC (LIKE AN ANIMAL) THE OTHER PEOPLE CAN TRY TO GUESS WHAT YOUR CONSTELLATION IS.

MAKING PAPER AIRPLANES AND TRYING TO MAKE LOOPS, OR SEEING WHICH ONE GOES THE FARTHEST IS FUN AND DOESN'T USUALLY BREAK TOO MANY THINGS.

WHEN THE KIDS WERE YOUNGER, DOING SKITS, SOME MADE UP, SOME BIBLE STORIES. THEY WOULD SET UP A "THEATER" IN THE LIVING ROOM WITH SEATS FOR THE AUDIENCE, PROPS, AND CANDLES OR LAMPS FOR APPROPRIATE LIGHTING.

STARGAZING - WE SOMETIMES USE OUR SON'S SMALL TELESCOPE BUT MOSTLY JUST THE NAKED EYE. WE MOSTLY DO THIS AT SPECIAL TIMES - WHEN JUPITER IS PARTICULARLY BRIGHT OR SOMETHING ELSE OF INTEREST TO SEE/LOOK FOR. WE FAIRLY FREQUENTLY CAN SEE A SHOOTING STAR AND SOMETIMES THE INTERNATIONAL SPACE STATION FLYING BY OVERHEAD. IT'S REFRESHING TO LOOK UP INTO THE NIGHT SKY. IT PROVIDES A SENSE OF CALM AND PEACEFULNESS AND HELPS US TO APPRECIATE AND REFOCUS ON OUR AWESOME CREATOR GOD THE FATHER.

WE SOMETIMES HAVE OUR OWN TALENT SHOW. EVERYONE HAS TO SHOW OFF ONE TALENT NO MATTER HOW SILLY.

WE USE THE HALLWAY AS A VOLLEYBALL COURT. WE TAPE BLUETAK TO NEWSPAPER SO IT LOOKS LIKE A NET (LIGHTWEIGHT) AND BOUNCE BALLOONS OVER IT. THE TALLER PEOPLE KNEEL SO THAT THE SMALLER PEOPLE CAN COMPETE. MIX IN BOTH TEAMS, ADULTS AND CHILDREN.

WE DO TARGET SHOOTING WITH BB GUNS.

WE HAVE HAD A LOT OF FUN MAKING A "RESTAURANT" AT HOME. THE KIDS CREATE A MENU, AND MAKE IT ON A FOLDED CARD. THEY MAKE A SIGN WITH THE NAME OF OUR RESTAURANT AND SET THE TABLE, ETC. THEY CREATE THE ATMOSPHERE WITH MUSIC PLAYING, LIGHTS DOWN LOW, CANDLES, ETC. THE PARENTS AND OLDER KIDS MAKE THE FOOD / COOK THE MEAL. EVERYONE GETS DRESSED UP AS IF WE ARE "GOING OUT" FOR DINNER, AND THEN WE ENJOY! WE TAKE TURNS BEING THE HOSTESS, WAITER, ETC. DON'T FORGET TO LEAVE A TIP!

MY CHILDREN LOVE TO PLAY HIDE-AND-SEEK IN THE DARK WITH THEIR DAD. THE LIGHTS GO OUT, AND DAD HIDES, AND THE CHILDREN ALL SEEK. THE CHILDREN HIDE, AND DAD SEEKS. MY FAMILY PLAYS WITH 'ROAMING' RULES — YOU DO NOT HAVE TO STAY PUT IN ONE PLACE, YOU CAN MOVE FROM ROOM TO ROOM TO ELUDE BEING FOUND!

DRAWING ON THE SIDEWALK WITH SIDEWALK CHALK. GIVE A THEME; AND LET EVERYONE GIVE THEIR INTERPRETATION. GIVE A PRIZE, OR SEVERAL PRIZES, FOR SOME ASPECT OF THE THEME INTERPRETATION. RECORD THE EVENT IN PHOTOS/WORDS IN SCRAPBOOK. REPEAT IT THE NEXT YEAR, AND NEXT. RE-LIVE FUN EXPERIENCES. LET PASSERBY'S STOP AND JOIN IN THE FUN IF DESIRED, OR LET THEM QUICKLY JUDGE "WINNERS". DRINK LOTS OF LEMONADE WHILE DRAWING. BEST DONE THE DAY BEFORE A BIG RAINSTORM, WHICH WILL "ERASE" THE CHALK AND "CLEAN THE MESS" WITHOUT ANY EFFORT ON YOUR PART. OR, LET THE KIDS CLEAN IT WITH A HOSE. (THAT MAY BE AS MUCH FUN AS DRAWING IT WAS...)

WE HAVE A GAME NIGHT, AND SOMETIMES INVITE OTHER FAMILIES TO JOIN US. WHEN YOU HAVE A LOT OF PEOPLE, A FUN GAME TO PLAY IS "THE RED CUP GAME". EVERYONE SITS AROUND THE TABLE, AND HAS A RED PLASTIC CUP, AND SOME SCRAP PAPER. EVERYONE COMES UP WITH THEIR OWN QUESTION OF, "WHO IN THIS GROUP IS MOST LIKELY TO…" AFTER THE QUESTIONS IS WRITTEN AND IS HANGING OFF THE TOP OF THE CUP, THE CUPS ARE PLACED INT THE CENTER. MIX THE CUPS UP SOME, AND THEN EVERYONE TAKES A CUP AND ANSWERS THE QUESTION ON DIFFERENT PIECE OF SCRAP PAPER AND PUT IT INSIDE THE CUP AND PASSES IT TO THE NEXT PERSON, AND SO ON AND SO ON, UNTIL YOU GET TO YOUR FIRST QUESTION AGAIN. THEN THE RESPONSES ARE READ. SOMETIMES IT STARTS OUT SLOW, BUT ONCE YOU GET THE HANG OF IT THE QUESTIONS GET BETTER AND THE RESPONSES GET FUNNIER. WE HAVE MADE SOME GOOD FRIENDS WITH THIS GAME (BUT BE CAREFUL IT COULD GO THE OTHER WAY ALSO)

WE ENJOY PLAYING A LOT OF GAMES, INCLUDING RUMMIKUB, SKIPBO, SCRABBLE, WHERE IN THE WORLD?, BOGGLE, AND MORE. WE ALSO PERIODICALLY DO SOMETHING WE CALL "WHAT I LIKE ABOUT…" EACH PERSON IN THE FAMILY TAKES TURNS SAYING SOMETHING THEY LIKE ABOUT EACH OF THE OTHER FAMILY MEMBERS UNTIL EVERY PERSON HAS SAID SOMETHING NICE ABOUT EVERY OTHER PERSON. WE'VE CREATED BOARD GAMES TOGETHER ON THE COMPUTER AND THEN BROUGHT IT TO KINKO'S, BLEW IT UP AND LAMINATED IT. WE LOVE PLAYING GAMES WE'VE CREATED TOGETHER. WE ALSO LOVE TO DO "BEANIE BABY TOSS" USING KITCHEN BOWLS AND TOSSING OUR BEANIE BABIES INTO THEM. DRAWING AND COLORING TOGETHER IS ALWAYS A HIT. I LIKE TO DRAW GARDENS FOR MY KIDS. I DRAW LOTS OF STEMS WITH LEAVES ON THEM AND LEAVE IT TO THEM TO CREATE THE FLOWERS. THEN WE PUT IT UP IN OUR SCHOOLROOM. MY KIDS ARE 5 AND 7.

OUR FAVOURITE THING TO DO TOGETHER IS BOARD GAMES. WE HAVE FUN, LAUGH TOGETHER. IT TEACHES THE KIDS HOW TO PREFER ONE ANOTHER, WHEN THEY ALLOW A SIBLING TO CHOOSE A GAME THAT THEY MAY NOT WANT TO PLAY.

CREATE OWN GAMEBOARD GAMES WITH QUESTION CARDS AND TRICKS. AND AFTER TO PLAY IT ALL TOGETHER. IT IS FUN AND POSSIBLE TO TAKE CARE OF EVERYBODY'S SKILLS INTO ACCOUNT.

MORE ON BOARD GAMES:

HERE'S A LIST OF **" FAVORITE GAMES "** THAT CAME UP TIME AND AGAIN IN THE RESPONSES WE RECEIVED. MAYBE YOU CAN FIND A NEW FAMILY FAVORITE IN THIS LIST! CHECK THRIFT SHOPS, YARD SALES, ETC. AND YOU'LL UNCOVER SOME OF THESE — SUPER CHEAP!

APPLES TO APPLES

RUMMY

FOUR PLAYER CHECKERS

KINGS IN THE CORNER

CARD GAMES FROM MIND JOLT

DUTCH BLITZ

AGGRAVATION

LIFE

PAYDAY

CLUE

MONOPOLY

UNO

QUIRKLE

RACK-O

YAHTZEE

BLINK

WAR

CHESS

CHECKERS

BACKGAMMON

RISK

TRAIN DOMINOES

RUMMIKUB

And finally, a couple of game playing tips:

We have a lot of games so sometimes we will pull 3 off of the shelf. If more than half of us groan at the site of the game, everyone helps to verify that all parts are there then it is rubber banded and put in the give-away pile. If there are no real groans or only a few, we play the game. If it is not really being enjoyed we stop and do the same thing with it as the other. This has helped us to clean off many shelves over the past year. And it is a fun way to figure out if we want something besides making the whole family help out. Usually we end up with a great fun game.

One way we take the 'sting' out of losing is that the winner puts the game away, and if you didn't win, you get to pick the next game we play!

What games do you remember from when you were little? Introduce them to your kids and let them know you played this when you were their age. That makes it all the more fun for them!

Places to Explore in our Community:

Places to visit in our Region:

Day trips we have done,
and how they turned out:

Back Yard Activity Ideas:

Rainy Day Indoor Ideas:

PRACTICAL TIPS FOR MANAGING YOUR HOME AND HOMESCHOOLING TIME:

MAKE A SCHEDULE AND STICK TO IT THE BEST YOU CAN. DON'T ANSWER THE PHONE, AND PUT A SIGN ON THE FRONT DOOR SAYING THAT SCHOOL IS IN SESSION.

DO NOT: ...ANSWER THE PHONE... ...CHECK YOUR EMAIL... ...OPEN THE DOOR FOR THE WELL MEANING NEIGHBOR. DEVELOP ROUTINES FOR YOUR DAY THAT YOUR KIDS CAN DEPEND ON.

FINALLY LEARNING THAT LEARNING TRULY IS EVERYWHERE, AND MAKING THE EFFORT TO TEACH THROUGH EVERYTHING.

PLANNING, PLANNING, PLANNING. AN ANNUAL PLAN WORKS WELL, BECAUSE YOU KNOW WHAT YOUR GOALS ARE FOR YOUR CHILDREN AND YOU CAN MAKE EFFORT TO ACCOMPLISH THEM. IT DOESN'T ALWAYS MEAN THAT MY CHILD AND I ARE STRICT ABOUT FOLLOWING IT TO THE T, BUT IT DOES PROVIDE US A STRUCTURE TO WORK WITH. THIS HAS HELPED ME TO BE MORE HAPPY IN HOMESCHOOLING MY SON.

GETTING UP BEFORE THE CHILDREN TO HAVE MY QUIET TIME, SHOWER, AND EXERCISE. WE HAVE BIBLE FIRST WITH BREAKFAST AND OUR DAY SEEMS TO GO MUCH SMOOTHER SINCE WE HAVE ESTABLISHED OUR PRIORITIES.

YOUR FAMILY IS UNIQUE. YOUR SCHEDULE WILL (AND SHOULD) LOOK DIFFERENT THAN THAT OF ALL OTHER FAMILIES. GO OVER COMPLETED SCHOOLWORK ASAP. THIS PROVIDES IMMEDIATE FEEDBACK FOR STUDENTS AND AVOIDS HUGE PILES OF SCHOOLWORK TO CHECK/GRADE LATER. PREPARE LESSON PLANS AHEAD AS MUCH AS POSSIBLE. THEN REEVALUATE EACH WEEKEND TO ADJUST FOR NEEDS AND/OR ATTEMPT TO KEEP ON TRACK.

I SET A TIMER FOR WHEN I'M ONLINE. I ALSO KEEP A NOTE PAD WITH ME TO JOT DOWN THINGS I REMEMBERED THAT I NEED TO DO. I HAVE A BLOCK OF TIME BEFORE LUNCH AND AROUND 3:45 TO WORK ON MY PERSONAL TO-DO LIST, SO THE REMAINDER OF THE TIME, I'M WORKING WITH THE KIDS.

SAYING "NO!" IF I'M ASKED TO DO SOMETHING AND I DON'T FEEL THE LORD IS LEADING ME TO IT, OR I KNOW IT'S GOING TO AFFECT MY FAMILY IN A NEGATIVE WAY TIME WISE, I SAY NO.

NETWORK WITH OTHER FAMILIES AND USE EACH OTHER TO SHARE THE PROCESS (TEACH ONE ANOTHER'S' KIDS DIFFERENT THINGS).

GET THE HOUSEHOLD STUFF OUT OF THE WAY SO THAT EVERYONE CAN FOCUS ON LEARNING INSTEAD OF THE PILE OF DISHES OR LAUNDRY OR .... GET THE COOKING CHALLENGE OUT OF THE WAY - TEACH EVERYONE HOW TO GET THEIR OWN BREAKFAST, HAVE SOMEONE IN CHARGE OF A SIMPLE LUNCH AND DO BULK COOKING OR A COOKING EXCHANGE IN THE FREEZER FOR DINNER, USE THE SLOW COOKER ON THE DAYS YOU'LL BE OUT AND ABOUT. IF YOU CAN GET THESE TWO THINGS (HOUSEHOLD AND COOKING) UNDER CONTROL IT FREES UP A TON OF TIME AND HELPS EVERYONE FOCUS ON TEACHING/LEARNING.

'PRIORITY' SUGGESTS ONE THING. HAVING 5 THINGS ON YOUR PRIORITIES LIST DOESN'T WORK. MAKE SURE YOU ARE WORKING TOWARDS THE #1 GOAL I.E. SENTENCE STRUCTURE, AND THEN POOL OTHER THINGS AROUND IT. YOU'LL GO TO SLEEP KNOWING YOU WORKED ON THE TOP THING EVEN ON A HECTIC SERVICED JUMBLED DAY.

HAVE AS MUCH AS POSSIBLE DONE BEFORE YOU NEED IT--PENCILS SHARPENED, BOOKS AND WORKSHEETS EASILY ACCESSIBLE, SCHEDULE FOR THE DAY PRINTED OUT AND READY TO GO, ETC.

LET IT GO IF THEY ARE FRUSTRATED, COME BACK TO IT LATER, WEEKS LATER OR MAYBE MONTHS LATER, AND THEY WILL GET IT. RELAX, THEY LEARN ANYWAY.

IF I START MY DAY WITH GOD MY DAY AND TIME RUN SO MUCH SMOOTHER. I HAVE EXPERIMENTED AND THE DAYS I DON'T READ AND PRAY FIRST THING I AM FRUSTRATED AND FEEL OVERWHELMED. ALSO, I LEARNED FROM ANOTHER HOMESCHOOLER THIS. GOD HAS GIVEN US EACH THE SAME AMOUNT OF TIME. IF YOU WASTE THAT TIME YOU CAN'T GET IT BACK. SO WHEN THE CHILDREN WASTE THE TIME HAVE THEM DO SOMETHING FOR GOD FOR THAT SAME AMOUNT OF TIME.

SET THE TIMER SO YOU KNOW AND YOUR STUDENTS KNOW WHEN IT'S TIME TO STOP. SHORT LESSONS KEEP EVERYONE MOVING AND ATTENTIVE.

THE ONLY THING I HAVE DISCOVERED IS THAT IF WE DON'T START OUR 'SCHOOL' BY A SPECIFIC TIME OF THE DAY, IT ISN'T GOING TO HAPPEN. AS A FAMILY, WE HAVE TO BEGIN OUR SCHOOL WORK BY 10:30 OR IT'S ALL LOST. OUR SCHOOL TIME IS MORE PRODUCTIVE AND REWARDING WHEN I DON'T LET CHORES (SHOPPING, CLEANING, AND OTHER BUSYWORK) DISTRACT ME FROM BEING INVOLVED WITH THE LEARNING EXPERIENCE.

THE BEST THING I HAVE FOUND IS TO BE FLEXIBLE, AND TO MAKE HOMESCHOOLING FIT OUR LIVES, RATHER THAN THE OTHER WAY AROUND. WITH FIVE KIDS INVOLVED IN LOTS OF ACTIVITIES, WE FIND CREATIVE WAYS TO LEARN. THAT IS ONE REASON WHY AUDIOBOOKS WORK SO WELL. WE CAN TAKE THEM WITH US WHEN WE ARE ON THE GO. WE ALSO MAKE OUR FAMILY TIME AT HOME FUN. RATHER THAN JUST WATCH T.V., WE HAVE A FAMILY TIME A FEW NIGHTS A WEEK WHERE WE WATCH AN EDUCATIONAL MOVIE TOGETHER. THIS HAS BEEN FUN, AND EDUCATIONAL.

WE TRY TO GET UP EARLY AND GET SCHOOL DONE IN THE MORNING. THEN, IF "SOMETHING HAPPENS", WE HAVE AN OPPORTUNITY TO "CATCH UP" LATER IN THE DAY. WE DO NOT SCHEDULE ACTIVITIES OUTSIDE THE HOME UNTIL THE AFTERNOON OR EVENING.

BE SATISFIED WITH WHAT YOU DO GET FINISHED, AND ENJOY THE TIME WORKING ON IT. (AS OPPOSED TO CHECKING OFF BOXES ON A LIST OF COMPLETED ITEMS).

TURN ON THE PHONE ANSWERING MACHINE AND DO NOT PICK UP UNLESS IT IS AN EMERGENCY. CONSIDER JUST UNPLUGGING THE PHONE DURING SCHOOL TIME TO DECREASE THE TEMPTATION TO ANSWER INCOMING CALLS.

I KNOW THIS IS OBVIOUS BUT HOW MANY OF ACTUALLY DO THIS: PUTTING EVERYTHING IN ITS OWN PLACE AND A PLACE FOR EVERYTHING. DE-CLUTTERING IS ANOTHER BIG HELP. THE MORE STUFF YOU HAVE, THE MORE STUFF YOU HAVE TO TAKE CARE AND HAVE A PLACE FOR. THERE'S SO MUCH "STUFF" OUT THERE.... YOU CAN'T USE IT ALL. IF YOU CAN'T FIND A PLACE FOR IT - DO YOU REALLY NEED IT?

OLDER STUDENTS CAN DO A LOT OF WORK INDEPENDENTLY. TEACH THE SAME THING TO ALL OF THE STUDENTS - JUST AT DIFFERENT LEVELS. HAVE A LIST OF INDEPENDENT THINGS EVEN YOUNGER CHILDREN CAN DO ON THEIR OWN SO THAT THEY CAN USE THEIR TIME PRODUCTIVELY IF THEY FINISH EARLY OR YOU ARE OTHERWISE NOT AVAILABLE AT THAT MOMENT.

STREAMLINE AS MUCH AS POSSIBLE. I TRY TO WORK OUT A PLAN WHERE I CAN KEEP ALL THE NEEDED RECORDS ON ALL THE CHILDREN IN ONE PLACE SO THAT I'M NOT HAVING TO SWITCH FROM ONE BOOK TO ANOTHER OR HAVING TO TRANSFORM INFORMATION FROM ONE METHOD TO ANOTHER. I LOOK AT THE WAYS THE INFORMATION NEEDS TO BE REPORTED TO SATISFY ANY STATE REQUIREMENTS AS WELL AS ANY OTHER THINGS WE NEED TO REPORT (LIKE HIGH SCHOOL CREDITS, ETC.) AND TRY TO MAKE THE RECORDING OF THE INFORMATION AS SIMPLE AS POSSIBLE.

I HAVE A POSTED SCHEDULE FOR EVERY MEMBER OF THE FAMILY INCLUDING 1/2 HOUR SEGMENTS FOR ALL SUBJECTS AND CHORES. MANY SUBJECTS DO NOT TAKE THE FULL HALF HOUR SO THERE IS A LITTLE TIME TO ADD TO THOSE SUBJECTS WE WANT TO SPEND A LITTLE LONGER AT. IT ALSO HELPS TO HAVE THE KIDS UP, DRESSED, BEDS MADE AND READY FOR WHATEVER THE DAY HOLDS. THIS WAY THAT MAD RUSH TO GET EVERYONE DRESSED AND READY TO HEAD OUT THE DOOR DOES NOT HAPPEN.

WE USE DRIVING TIME FOR A LOT OF SCHOOLING. BOTH KIDS ARE EXPECTED TO HAVE A CURRENT BOOK THEY ARE READING WITH THEM IN THE CAR IF WE WILL BE IN THE CAR FOR MORE THAN 5 MINUTES. THE KIDS ALSO DO MATH OR SPANISH FLASHCARDS WITH EACH OTHER IN THE BACK SEAT WHILE I DRIVE. WE ALSO KEEP SMALL NOTEBOOKS BACK THERE FOR THEM TO WRITE DOWN ANY QUESTIONS THEY HAVE THAT MOMMY CAN'T ANSWER ON THE SPOT. THAT WAY WE DON'T FORGET TO LOOK THEM UP WHEN WE GET HOME!

IT ALWAYS HELPS US TREMENDOUSLY IF I LAY DOWN THE LAW AND SAY NO READING OR PLAYING UNTIL AFTER SCHOOL IS DONE. WE HAVE TO GET UP, DRESS, EAT, DO CHORES, AND GET RIGHT TO SCHOOL, OR ELSE THE MORNING DRAGS ON AND NOTHING IS ACCOMPLISHED OR DONE IN AN ORDERLY MANNER.

DON'T OVER PLAN WHAT CAN BE ACCOMPLISHED IN A DAY (IT ALWAYS TAKES LONGER THAN YOU THINK.)

SPEND ONE WEEK TO A MONTH IN THE SUMMER TO PLAN AND ORGANIZE THE WHOLE YEAR. IT SAVES LOTS OF TIME AND FRUSTRATION OF TRYING TO WING IT AS YOU GO. BE FLEXIBLE IN THAT SCHEDULE SO THAT AS LIFE HAPPENS IT DOES NOT CREATE A PANIC WHEN IT (AND IT WILL) INTERRUPTS YOUR SCHEDULE. IT WILL HAVE TO BE TWEAKED FROM TIME TO TIME.

FIRST OF ALL, I NEED TO STAY FOCUSED ON SCHOOL AND NOT GO OFF ON MY OWN RABBIT TRAILS. FOR EXAMPLE, IF WE'RE IN THE MIDDLE OF AN ASSIGNMENT, I'LL SOMETIMES SAY, "I'M GOING TO DO THIS (BIT OF HOUSEWORK OR INTERNET RESEARCH) WHILE YOU'RE WORKING ON THAT." BUT WHEN HE'S DONE I DON'T STOP WHAT I'M DOING TO MOVE HIM ON TO THE NEXT STEP/SUBJECT. NEXT THING I KNOW, I'VE "LOST" AN HOUR OR MORE OF THE DAY THAT CAN'T BE RE-CLAIMED. I HAVE TO START ANY NON-SCHOOL PROJECT WITH THE MIND-SET THAT I'M GOING TO STOP WHEN HE'S DONE WITH HIS ASSIGNMENT - EVEN IF I'M NOT DONE!

RELAX, RELAX, RELAX. THEY DON'T HAVE TO KNOW EVERY THERE IS TO KNOW. FOCUS ON THE ESSENTIAL BASICS. THE REST WILL COME IN TIME AS THEY GROW AND DEVELOP THEIR OWN INTERESTS ON THEIR OWN TIME. SETTING LONG AND SHORT TERM GOALS HELPS ME SEE THE BIG PICTURE. WE DO DAILY, WEEKLY YEARLY AND LONG RANGE (AFTER HIGH SCHOOL) GOALS.

1. MAKING LISTS AND PLANS AND SCHEDULES EVERY SINGLE DAY FOR THAT DAY AND DAYS AHEAD AND THEN KEEPING THEM HANDY FOR REFERENCE.

2. KEEPING A "MOM NOTEBOOK" AROUND ME AT ALL TIMES WITH LESSON PLANS, RECORD PAGES, LIST, SCHEDULES ETC. ALL IN ONE PLACE.

3. READ AHEAD OF THE KIDS: IE. READING ASSIGNMENTS, HISTORY BOOKS, SCIENCE BOOKS AND EXPERIMENTS. IN OTHER WORDS KNOW THE MATERIAL BEFORE YOUR CHILD VENTURES INTO IT! THIS SAVES YOU TIME DURING YOUR ACTUAL SCHOOL TIME AND ALSO IF YOU TRY TO MULTI-TASK WHILE KIDS WORK INDEPENDENTLY...YOU CAN ANSWER OR GIVE HELP QUICKLY AND EASILY.

4. KEEPING HOUSE CLEAN AND ORGANIZED IS A MUST. GREAT LEARNING USUALLY DOES NOT HAPPEN IN CHAOS...WHEN THINGS ARE ORGANIZED AND EASILY ACCESSIBLE, CHILDREN OR YOU CAN GRAB WHAT IS NEEDED FOR WHATEVER PROJECT IS ASSIGNED.

5. CLEAN UP IS A MUST AFTER EVERY PROJECT!

6. WE DO CHORES EVERY MORNING BEFORE SCHOOL AND EVERY NIGHT BEFORE BED TO KEEP THINGS RUNNING SMOOTHLY.

7. WE ALSO PREPARE OUR MEALS AS MUCH AHEAD AS POSSIBLE USING THE "ONCE-A-MONTH" COOKING CONCEPT.

8. JUST WAIT! I AM SUCH AN IMPULSE PERSON AND IT HAS BEEN VERY DIFFICULT FOR ME TO LEARN THAT WAITING CAN BE A VERY GOOD THING...NOT EVERY ISSUE OR THING HAS TO BE ADDRESSED THE MINUTE IT COMES UP. SOMETIMES TIME ITSELF CAN BE OUR BEST FRIEND.

9. WE TRY TO HAVE BLOCKS OF TIME FOR SCHOOL WHERE OTHERS ARE AWARE OF THOSE TIMES. IT DOESN'T ALWAYS WORK BUT IT HAS CUT BACK ON INTERRUPTIONS. I KEEP SAYING THAT ONE DAY I AM MAKING A SIGN TO HANG ON MY FRONT DOOR: "DO NOT DISTURB, SCHOOL IN PROCESS"...BUT I WORRY IT MAY APPEAR RUDE. I DO SEE A NEED HOWEVER TO PROTECT YOUR "SCHOOL TIME" TO SOME EXTENT.

10. EVEN THOUGH I LIST THIS LAST IT IS BY FAR THE MOST IMPORTANT KEY TO OUR HOMESCHOOL/LIFE SUCCESS. SEEK THE LORD'S HEART FOR YOUR DAY EVERYDAY! SEEK WHAT HE HAS PLANNED FOR YOU!!! START FRESH EVERY MORNING WITH HIM! NO MATTER

WHAT HAPPENED THE DAY BEFORE (LOSING YOUR TEMPER, GETTING IMPATIENT AND FRUSTRATED WITH A CHILD, NEGLECTING A NEED)...WHEREVER YOU FELL SHORT...LAY IT AT HIS FEET, ASK FORGIVENESS AND SEEK HIS STRENGTH TO NOT REPEAT IT THIS DAY! ASK FOR JOY!!! I REALLY THINK THE LORD LOVES TO GIVE US A JOYFUL HEART AND ATTITUDE!!! WHEN WE SPEND OUR FIRST FRUITS WITH HIM IN THE MORNING, HE SEEMS TO LINGER WITH US ALL THE REST OF THE DAY!!! AND HERE IS ANOTHER BIGGIE! PRAY FOR YOUR KIDS! REALLY, REALLY PRAY FOR YOUR KIDS!!!! ASK THE LORD TO SHOW YOU WHAT YOU NEED TO BE TO THEM THAT DAY...ASK FOR HIS WISDOM AHEAD OF TIME AND HIS EYES TO SEE. LAY THEIR ATTITUDES OR SHORTCOMING AT HIS FEET AND SEEK HIS HEART WITH HOW TO APPROACH OR REPROACH. I RECENTLY PUT A SIGN UP OVER MY KITCHEN WINDOW THAT I PAINTED ONTO AN OLD RECLAIMED PIECE OF WOOD: "THY HEART, LORD WILL I SEEK!" IT REMINDS ME TO SEEK HIS FACE FIRST THING EVERYDAY!!!

I HAVE ADOPTED SHORT LESSONS, AND I'VE LOOKED FOR CURRICULUM THAT IS EASY TO UNDERSTAND AND DOES NOT INVOLVE A LOT OF TEACHER PREPARATION. I ALSO HAVE ELIMINATED BUSY WORK - ALL SCHOOL WORK HAS TO HAVE PURPOSE!

I TRY TO START THE MORE CHALLENGING SUBJECTS AND END WITH THE MORE ENJOYABLE (I.E. READ-ALOUDS). I HAVE LEARNED WHAT GETS LEFT TO LAST, UNLESS WE REALLY WANT TO DO IT, DOES NOT GET DONE.

TAKING THE TIME TO PLAN OUT OUR STUDY SCHEDULE SAVES ME LOTS OF TIME. I BEGIN TO DO THIS BEFORE OUR STUDY YEAR BEGINS BY 1) GETTING THE CALENDAR FOR THE YEAR DONE; 2) COPYING THE TABLE OF CONTENTS FROM EACH TEXT AND WRITING THE DATES FOR EACH CHAPTER; 3) PLACING ALL THIS INFORMATION ONTO MY DATABASE SO THAT I GET A WEEKLY SCHEDULE. GOD WORKED 6 DAYS AND RESTED ON THE 7TH, SO WE WORK FOR 6 WEEKS AND REST ON THE 7TH. WE BEGIN OUR STUDY YEAR IN MID-AUGUST AND FINISH EARLY JUNE. WE DON'T FOLLOW THIS SCHEDULE AT CHRISTMAS (WE REST AFTER 5 WEEKS FOR 2 WEEKS) AND AT THE END OF THE YEAR (WE WORK FOR 7 WEEKS THEN START VACATION). WE FIND THAT WE DON'T GET BURNED OUT.

TEACHING MY CHILDREN TO BE ABLE TO DO THEIR WORK ON THEIR OWN, ONLY ASKING FOR HELP WHEN THEY AREN'T ABLE TO FIND ANSWERS ON THEIR WON.

TREAT IT LIKE A 'REAL' JOB/CAREER (BECAUSE THAT'S WHAT IT TRULY IS)! TAKE IT VERY SERIOUSLY. I KNOW THIS MAY SOUND SILLY TO SOME, HOWEVER, I FELL INTO THE TRAP OF THINKING THAT BECAUSE WE SCHOOL AT HOME, WHERE IT IS LAID BACK, THAT I COULD BE LAID BACK ABOUT GETTING AROUND TO SCHOOLING! I WOULD SUGGEST TO ANYONE NOT ALREADY DOING SO TO SET BECOME ULTRA-ORGANIZED WITH YOUR TIME. JUST PUT YOURSELF IN THE MINDSET OF A TEACHER WHO WORKS OUT IN THE PUBLIC/PRIVATE SECTOR. RISE EARLY, PLAN AHEAD FOR EVERYTHING, SHOWER AND DRESS AND EAT A GOOD BREAKFAST THEN GET GOING WITH SCHOOL. I HAVE TO SCHOOL EARLY OTHERWISE IT NEVER GETS DONE. MAKE SOME PREPARATIONS THE NIGHT BEFORE. FIND MATERIALS AND RESOURCES AND HAVE THEM PREPPED. TURN OFF THE PHONE DURING LESSON TIME. CONSIDER SCHOOL TIME A NON-NEGOTIABLE APPOINTMENT. DO NOT OVERESTIMATE YOUR ABILITY TO MULTITASK - THE KIDS ARE USUALLY THE LOSERS ON THAT ONE.

NO ELECTRONICS (VIDEO GAMES, COMPUTERS, MUSIC) FOR THE KIDS UNTIL AFTER THEY HAVE COMPLETED THEIR SCHOOL WORK FOR THE DAY. THIS IS A MUST!

CHOOSING SPECIFIC DAYS FOR SPECIFIC TASKS. TUESDAY IS FLOOR DAY, MONDAY IS SHEETS AND TOWELS DAY, ETC. KNOWING MY OWN BIO-RHYTHMS AND WORKING WITH THEM. I DO MY THINKING IN THE MORNING, MY PHYSICAL ACTIVITY IN THE AFTERNOON. WRITING ALL TASKS DOWN, AND THEM ASSIGNING THEM AN ACTION STEP ON MY CALENDAR. IF THEY AREN'T TURNED INTO AN ACTION, THEY DON'T GET DONE!

ESTABLISH A ROUTINE AND STICK TO IT AS MUCH AS POSSIBLE. POST YOUR SCHEDULE AND BE SURE EVERYONE UNDERSTANDS WHAT MUST BE DONE WHEN. IT'S TAKEN YEARS FOR MY CHILDREN TO MAKE THE ROUTINES A HABIT, BUT WHEN THEY FINALLY DO, IT'S A HUGE LOAD OFF OF ME.

KEEP LIFE SIMPLE, EVEN MINIMAL. EXPECTATIONS NEED TO BE SIMPLE, OUTSIDE COMMITMENTS NEED TO BE MINIMAL. SIMPLE ISN'T THE SAME AS EASY OR LAZY, WHEN YOU KEEP THINGS SIMPLE YOU CAN BE FLEXIBLE IN HOW YOU MEET GOALS ESPECIALLY SCHOOL GOALS.

I HAVE FOUND THAT BY MAKING A GRID FOR EACH CHILD AT THE BEGINNING OF THE YEAR THAT HAS ALL OF THE CHILD'S SUBJECTS LISTED DOWN ONE SIDE AND A COLUMN FOR EACH DAY OF THE WEEK, I AM ABLE TO QUICKLY WRITE OUT EACH WEEK'S ASSIGNMENTS. I JUST PRINT OUT A COPY FOR EACH WEEK ON CARD STOCK (OTHERWISE THEY TEAR OUT OF A THREE RING BINDER TOO EASILY), THREE HOLE PUNCH IT, AND PUT THEM IN A 3-RING BINDER. EACH WEEK I CAN LOOK AT WHAT WAS COMPLETED THE PREVIOUS WEEK AND WRITE IN THE NEW ASSIGNMENTS. THE CHILDREN CHECK OFF THE WORK AS IT IS COMPLETED.

1. TEACH DISCIPLINE FIRST AND FOREMOST. ALL STUDIES COME TO A HALT WHEN AN ATTITUDE OR DISCIPLINE PROBLEM ARISES.

2. GIVE EACH CHILD SOME 1 ON 1 TIME - EVEN THE LITTLEST. IN FACT START WITH THE LITTLEST SO THEY GET THEIR "TANK FILLED" AND CAN GO PLAY.

3. HAVE THE "FREE" SCHOOL AGE CHILD PLAY WITH THE LITTLE ONES WHILE ANOTHER SCHOOL AGER DOES SCHOOL. SHOW THEM HOW TO PLAY NICELY, WHEN TO COME TO YOU FOR HELP, GIVE THEM AN APPROPRIATE LIST OF THINGS THAT THEY CAN DO WHILE YOU ARE BUSY TEACHING.

SET ASIDE EVERYTHING ELSE AND DEVOTE YOUR TIME TO HOMESCHOOLING. DON'T TRY TO HOMESCHOOL AND RUN YOUR BUSINESS DURING THE SAME PERIOD OF TIME, OR GET HOUSEWORK DONE, OR REPLY TO EMAILS. JUST FOCUS ON ONE THING...HOMESCHOOLING.

BE UP AND READY TO GO, INCLUDING BREAKFAST AND WORK TO BE DONE LAID OUT, BEFORE THE KIDS AWAKE.

MY BIGGEST TIP IS TO ESTABLISH A WRITTEN DAILY ROUTINE, THAT CAN BE FOLLOWED THROUGH ON, FOR MOST DAYS, EVEN IN OTHER ENVIRONMENTS, OR IF LIFE GETS BUSY WITH OTHER THINGS. CONSIDER AGREEING ON THIS ROUTINE AS A FAMILY AND GETTING A WRITTEN COMMITMENT FROM EACH MEMBER THEY ARE IN AGREEMENT. WE CURRENTLY HAVE OUR SCHEDULE STEPPED OUT ON A BIG POSTER AND THIS BIG FORMAT HAS BEEN VERY HELPFUL! IT IS IMPERATIVE TO ESTABLISH A SENSE OF ACCOMPLISHMENT AND ACCOUNTABILITY WITH HOMESCHOOLING CHILDREN. THEY MAY NOT HAVE A "DUE DATE" FOR THAT WRITTEN REPORT. HOWEVER, TEACH EARLY THAT SCHOOL IS PRIORITY AND NEEDS TO BE DONE BEFORE MOVING ON TO OTHER THINGS. BE CLEAR BUT REALISTIC WITH YOUR EXPECTATIONS.

REWARD GOOD EFFORT AND SUCCESSES WHENEVER ABLE. WITHHOLD PRIVILEGES IF "DIDDLE DADDLING" OCCURS... YOURSELF INCLUDED!

THE MOST HELPFUL TIP FOR MANAGING OUR HOMESCHOOLING TIME IS TO MAP OUT OUR WORLD VIEW AND CONTINUE TO BRING OUR SCHOOL SUBJECTS BACK TO THAT. IT HELPS ME AS THE TEACHER NOT TO GET SIDE TRACKED.

FOR A WHILE IT WORKED TO HAVE AN OLDER CHILD WORKING WITH OR TAKING CARE OF A YOUNGER CHILD WHILE I WORKED WITH ANOTHER. AND THEN HAVE THEM TRADE OFF. NOW THE OLDEST REALLY NEED THAT TIME TO GET SOME INDEPENDENT WORK DONE. THEY STILL HELP WITH THE YOUNGER BUT NOT FOR AS BIG A CHUNK OF TIME. ABSOLUTELY LOOK AT IT AS A JOB-I CAN'T TALK ON THE PHONE OR ALLOW OTHERS TO STEAL MY TIME. IF I MUST STEP AWAY-HAVE SOMETHING ALREADY PREPARED FOR THEM TO DO WHILE YOU'RE GONE - A PAGE ON MULTIPLICATION, WORK ON PENMANSHIP, FINISH THE SENTENCES YOU NEVER GOT TO, ETC. ANYTHING THEY CAN DO ON THEIR OWN. TRAIN THEM TO BE RESPONSIBLE WHEN THEY SEE YOU STEP AWAY IT MEANS, I'VE GOT WORK TO DO, AND HOLD THEM ACCOUNTABLE TO IT. ON YOUR END, MAKE IT SHORT AND QUICK AND TRAIN YOUR FAMILY AND FRIENDS BY NOT ANSWERING THE PHONE DURING SCHOOL TIME. WHEN YOU DO RETURN THE CALL, EXPLAIN YOU COULDN'T ANSWER THE PHONE BECAUSE YOU WERE IN THE MIDDLE OF SCHOOL.

SEPARATE THE KIDS WHEN THEY ARE WORKING INDEPENDENTLY AND IN ONE OF THOSE HARASS EACH OTHER MOODS.

GETTING A GOOD NIGHT'S SLEEP SO I CAN COPE BETTER WITH THE NEXT DAY. I WISH IT WAS EASIER TO PRACTICE.

EVERYONE MUST BE DRESSED WITH CHORES DONE PRIOR TO BREAKFAST. IF I RELAX ON THIS POLICY, IT IS TOO HARD TO GET MY KIDS BACK TOGETHER TO BEGIN BIBLE STUDY OR SCHOOL.

RELAX! REMEMBER THE BIG PICTURE AND LOVE THEM, LIVE LIFE WITH THEM, AND DO THE WORK TOGETHER. EVEN IF YOU DON'T DO EVERY BOOK/CURRICULUM, THE ATMOSPHERE MAKES EVERYTHING WORK TOGETHER BETTER.

PLANNING MEALS AND HAVING A BASIC SCHEDULE. I'M NOT THE GREATEST AT THIS, BUT IT IS ONE OF MY GOALS FOR THIS NEXT SCHOOL YEAR.

BOOKMARK ALL THE SITES YOU FIND THAT ARE RELATED TO HOMESCHOOLING OR DOCUMENT THEM IN SOME WAY... BECAUSE YOU NEVER KNOW WHEN YOU WILL NEED IT.

I SET THE TONE FOR THE AMOUNT OF WORK THAT GETS DONE IN A DAY. IF I GET UP AND AM READY FOR THE DAY BEFORE THE KIDS ARE OUT OF BED, I CAN TACKLE QUITE A BIT OF MY TO-DO LIST. ALSO, WHEN THE KIDS GET UP AND SEE ME WORKING, THEY ARE MORE LIKELY TO GET THEIR MORNING CHORES DONE AND THEIR SCHOOLWORK STARTED ON TIME.

HAVE EVERYONE CHIP IN AND HELP WHEN THINGS NEED TO GET DONE. THIS SAVES LOTS OF TIME!

I LIKE TO HAVE OUR EVENINGS FREE FROM SCHOOL ACTIVITIES. I THINK WE ALL NEED A BREAK TO ENJOY EACH OTHER AS FAMILY, SEPARATE FROM SCHOOL.

A ROUTINE WORKS BETTER THAN A SCHEDULE. GO WITH WHAT WORKS FOR YOUR FAMILY AND DON'T TRY AND BE ANOTHER FAMILY. IF YOU ARE LATE RISERS GO WITH THAT (IT'S ONE OF THE BENEFITS OF HOMESCHOOLING), IF YOU HAVE NIGHT OWLS, GO WITH THAT. IF YOU HAVE A SCHEDULE YOU USUALLY ALWAYS FEEL BEHIND (AND UNSUCCESSFUL) IF YOU HAVE A ROUTINE IT'S MORE FLEXIBLE AND SOME REALLY COOL LEARNING SERENDIPITIES CAN COME FROM THAT.

EVERY MORNING DO A LOAD OF LAUNDRY. EVERY EVENING RUN THE DISHWASHER. EVERY EVENING FOLD, EVERY MORNING PUT THE DISHES AWAY. YOU WILL NOT HAVE THE GUILT OF THE LAUNDRY PILE OR DISHES IN THE SINK. :)

HAVE A PLACE FOR EVERYTHING AND THEN PEOPLE CAN PUT EVERYTHING IN ITS PLACE. BE CREATIVE IF YOU DON'T HAVE MUCH ROOM. A DRESSER BY THE DOOR FOR EVERYONES MITTENS, HATS AND SCARVES DURING THE WINTER. A DRESSER FOR TOYS - EACH CHILD HAVING A DRAWER FOR THEIR SPECIAL THINGS. I ALWAYS WATCH AND ASK HOW OTHER FAMILIES DO THINGS AND JUDGE IF THOSE IDEAS WOULD WORK IN OUR HOME. SOME WON'T BECAUSE OF THE WAY OUR HOUSE IS BUT OTHERS WORK WELL.

I HAVE FOUND IN OUR HOME THAT I HAVE A VERY HIGH STANDARD. STANDARDS ARE GOOD, BUT NEED TO BE REALISTIC. SIT DOWN, LOOK AT WHAT TAKES SO MUCH TIME AND SEE IF IT CAN BE MODIFIED. DON'T LOOK AT WHAT OTHERS ARE DOING, DO WHAT WORKS FOR YOUR FAMILY.

DON'T BE A PROCRASTINATOR OR A PERFECTIONIST. NEITHER MENTALITY WORKS IN A HOMESCHOOL ENVIRONMENT. ACTUALLY, BEING A PERFECTIONIST LEADS TO THE PROCRASTINATOR, SO THEY'RE REALLY THE SAME THING. IF SOMETHING GOES WRONG ONCE, DON'T HOLD BACK FROM TRYING IT AGAIN BECAUSE YOU'RE AFRAID IT WON'T BE PERFECT.

TEACHING CHILDREN TO HELP AROUND THE HOUSE AND REQUIRING THEY DO SO HELPS THE FAMILY RUN EFFICIENTLY.

DO AS MUCH PLANNING OR SCHEDULING DURING THE SUMMER AS POSSIBLE.

BE FLEXIBLE, AND LOWER YOUR STANDARDS. YOU ARE BUSY EDUCATING YOUR KIDS. LIFE HAPPENS. DON'T SWEAT IT. SO WHAT IF YOUR HOUSE DOESN'T LOOK LIKE A FRIEND OR RELATIVE'S, WHO ISN'T HOMESCHOOLING. YOU'VE GOT KIDS HOME ALL DAY, EVERY DAY. SEE IT FOR THE BLESSING IT IS, AND DON'T GET STRESSED OUT ABOUT KEEPING YOUR HOUSE SPOTLESS. LOOK AT ALL THE GREAT LEARNING GOING ON!

YOU DON'T HAVE TO DO IT ALL. CUT OUT THE EXTRAS THAT ARE ONLY STRESSING YOU OUT.

RUN THE DISHWASHER (IF YOU HAVE ONE) EVERY SINGLE EVENING! THE CHILDREN PUT THE DISHES AWAY IN THE MORNING BEFORE BREAKFAST. AN EMPTY DISHWASHER IN THE MORNING REALLY HELPS OUR KITCHEN STAY TIDY THROUGHOUT THE DAY.

HAVE OLDER CHILDREN TEACH YOUNGER CHILDREN. THEY ACTUALLY ENJOY THIS. HAVING THE CHILDREN HAVE SET CHORES FOR A PERIOD OF TIME. MY CHILDREN GET CHORES BY THEIR AGE. WHEN THEY GET TO A CERTAIN AGE THEY GRADUATE TO A MORE DIFFICULT CHORE. THEY ACTUALLY LOOK FORWARD TO IT. THEY ALSO TEACH THE YOUNGER SIBLING COMING ON HOW TO DO THAT CHORE AND MENTOR THEM FOR A WHILE, BEFORE MOVING ON.

MAKE SURE YOU GET PLENTY OF REST AT NIGHT. MOST IMPORTANT - DON'T FORGET TO SPEND SOME QUIET TIME WITH THE LORD!

STREAMLINE YOUR TEACHING. YOU MAY THINK USING A LOT OF DIFFERENT PRE-CANNED CURRICULA IS TIME SAVING, BUT EACH HAS A DIFFERENT UNDERLYING PHILOSOPHY AND METHOD OF DOING THINGS. DEVELOPING YOUR OWN PHILOSOPHY AND DERIVING A METHODOLOGY FROM IT WILL GIVE A UNIFIED WAY OF EDUCATING TO YOUR HOME AND YOU CAN FOCUS ON THE ACTUAL STUDIES, RATHER THAN FIGURING OUT HOW TO DO THEM.

MAKE SCHOOL FUN UP TO A POINT...SAVES ON FIGHTS. TEACH YOUR CHILDREN THE ART OF BEING BEST FRIENDS, INSTEAD OF LISTENING TO ALL THE BICKERING. ALL THIS ROBS YOU OF YOUR TIME WITH THEM AND GETTING WHAT YOU NEED DONE TOO.

TRY NOT TO GET OVERWHELMED. IF YOU DON'T GET EVERY SINGLE THING DONE YOU HAD PLANNED FOR THAT DAY, SO WHAT. IT ONLY MEANS GOD HAD OTHER PLANS FOR YOU THAT DAY, AND WE ALL KNOW HE NEVER MAKES MISTAKES. SO SIT BACK AND THANK HIM FOR HELPING YOU REMEMBER WHO IS IN-CHARGE AND WHY YOU DECIDED TO HOMESCHOOL IN THE FIRST PLACE.

A TRIED AND TRUE ONE--HAVE A HOME FOR EVERYTHING AND IN ITS HOME IT SHOULD BE WHEN NOT IN USE.

WATCH THAT YOUR GOALS AND EXPECTATIONS FOR YOUR CHILDREN ARE DIFFERENT. MY GOAL IS THAT SOMEDAY THEY WILL BE ABLE TO DO THEIR CHORES INDEPENDENTLY, BUT MY EXPECTATION IS THAT THEY WILL NEED REMINDERS AND HELP FOR NOW.

PIN SOCKS TOGETHER WITH LARGE SAFETY PIN BEFORE PUTTING THEM IN DIRTY LAUNDRY (WITH 9 KIDS THIS IS A MUST - NO MORE SORTING SOCKS!!)

DON'T THINK YOU NEED TO DO 6.5 HOURS OF SCHOOL LIKE THE PUBLIC SCHOOLS. MUCH OF THEIR DAY IT WAITING IN LINE AND PLAYING, AND TEACHERS STILL USE TIME KILLING ACTIVITIES LIKE COLORING SHEETS. WHEN YOU TAKE OUT ALL OF THE WASTED TIME IN PUBLIC SCHOOLS, IT IS PROBABLY LESS THAN 3 HOURS OF INSTRUCTIONAL TIME AT THE ELEMENTARY LEVEL.

ELIMINATING/LIMITING SPORTS AND TV/MOVIES ALLOWS YOUR KIDS MORE TIME TO EXPLORE AND LEARN AND GIVES FAMILIES MORE TIME TO SPEND TOGETHER OR TO DO THINGS FOR OTHERS.

TOYS!! THEY REPRODUCE AND MULTIPLY REGULARLY!!SOME TIMES ALL WE HAVE TIME TO DO IS THROW EVERYTHING IN A TRASH BAG AND PUT IT IN THE GARAGE (WHERE WE KEEP OUR BUCKETS OF SORTED TOYS). THEN ON A RAINY DAY: SORT THEM INTO THEIR PROPER CONTAINERS! UNTIL THEN THE KIDS DON'T GET TO DIG IN THE BAGS TO FIND STUFF THEY WANT. IN THE WINTER THEY HAVE TO WAIT A LONG TIME AS THE GARAGE IS UN-HEATED!

I LEARNED THAT THE BIGGEST OBSTACLE TO GETTING MY WORK DONE WAS NOT LACK OF TIME OR ENERGY, BUT THE AMOUNT OF "STUFF" THAT I HAVE ALLOWED INTO MY HOUSE. IT IS EASY TO CLEAN A SPACE THAT HAS NO CLUTTER.

SIMPLIFY YOUR LIFE! GET RID OF KNICK-KNACKS, GLEAN ALL THE UNUSED CLOTHES, LIMIT TOYS ETC. THE LESS YOU HAVE, THE LESS YOU MUST MAINTAIN. WHAT REALLY BLESSES THE LIFE OF YOUR FAMILY AND WHAT JUST TAKES UP YOUR TIME IN MAINTENANCE?

I AM A LIST MAKER! I HAVE AN ERASABLE BOARD ON THE FRIDGE. ALL IMPORTANT STUFF FOR THE DAY CAN BE JOTTED DOWN THERE. SOMEHOW WITH BOLD MARKER, I DON'T FORGET THINGS AS EASILY AS WHEN IT IS NOT WRITTEN DOWN.

TEND TO SMALL PROBLEMS AS THEY OCCUR SO THEY DON'T GROW INTO BIG ONES!

EARLY TO BED, EARLY TO RISE. JUST GETTING UP A HALF AN HOUR BEFORE THE REST OF THE FAMILY, GETTING DRESSED TO YOUR SHOES, AND SPENDING A LITTLE QUIET, PEACEFUL TIME WITH THE LORD, CREATES AN ATMOSPHERE IN YOUR HOME THAT FOSTERS A GOOD DAY.

FOR PORTFOLIOS, HAVE THE KIDS GO THROUGH THEIR WORK FROM THE WEEK ON FRIDAY AND PICK ONE PIECE FROM EACH REQUIRED SUBJECT THEY WOULD LIKE TO INCLUDE IN THE PORTFOLIO - AT THE END OF THE YEAR YOU WILL HAVE ABOUT 36 EXAMPLES TO CHOOSE FROM TO INCLUDE AND YOUR WORK IS ALMOST DONE BY THE END OF THE YEAR - INSTEAD OF WAITING UNTIL THE LAST MINUTE!

GET HELP. ENLIST GRANDPARENTS, AUNTS, UNCLES, FRIENDS, DISTANT COUSINS. IF YOU ARE TEACHING A TOPIC WHERE YOU KNOW SOMEONE WHO IS AN EXPERT, GET YOUR KIDS SOME TIME WITH THEM. FOSTER INDEPENDENCE WITH YOUR KIDS' SCHOOL WORK AND ALLOW OTHER CAREGIVERS TO MANAGE THEM AND THEIR SCHOOLING FOR A DAY HERE AND THERE. YOU'LL BE AMAZED AT HOW MUCH THEY GET DONE WHEN THEY ARE GIVEN THE OWNERSHIP OF IT. AND, I'VE FOUND THAT IF GRANDPARENTS ARE ASKED TO HELP, THEY ARE MUCH MORE POSITIVE ABOUT HOMESCHOOLING, WHICH IS PASSED ON TO THE KIDS.

BREAK LARGE JOBS INTO SMALL CHUNKS SO THAT YOU ARE NOT OVERWHELMED. EVERY LITTLE HELPS.

MAKE SURE YOUR CHILDREN KNOW WHAT THEY CAN DO TO HELP AROUND THE HOUSE. THEY SHOULD HAVE THEIR OWN CHORES TO DO SO THEY ARE CONTRIBUTING MEMBERS OF THE HOUSEHOLD. IT IS SO IMPORTANT TO TEACH THEM THESE RESPONSIBILITIES WHILE THEY ARE YOUNG.

COOK IN A CROCKPOT. GREAT TIME SAVER — DINNER IS COOKING WHILE YOU ARE DOING OTHER ACTIVITIES. AT LEAST ONCE A WEEK PUT ON THE CROCK POT RIGHT AFTER BREAKFAST AND NOT HAVE TO THINK ABOUT DINNER!

ALL WINDEX IS DONE ON SAME DAY. ALL SWIFFERING AND VACUUMING IS DONE ONE SAME DAY. KIDS HAVE THE SAME CHORES FOR A ENTIRE YEAR SO THERE IS NO QUESTION WHO IS SUPPOSE TO DO THAT CHORE. THEN THEY TRAIN NEXT YOUNGEST CHILD TO DO THEIR CHORE FOR A FEW WEEKS, THEN IT IS NOW THE YOUNGER CHILD'S CHORE FOR ONE YEAR. WE CHANGE CHORES AT SUMMER TIME SO THE LEARNING CURVE IS DURING THE SUMMER NOT SCHOOL TIME.

ALWAYS REMEMBER THAT THERE WILL BE DAYS WHERE A SCHEDULE/ROUTINE JUST DON'T HAPPEN...DON'T GET DOWN ON YOURSELF BECAUSE OF THOSE OCCASIONAL DAYS

HANG IN THERE, DAY AFTER TOMORROW ALL THE KIDS WILL BE GONE AND YOU WILL MISS THESE HECTIC DAYS.

DO YOUR BEST TO CARVE OUT SOME "ME" TIME EVEN IF IT'S ONLY FOR 15 TO 30 MIN. A DAY. IT HELPS TO REJUVENATE YOU AND MAKES YOU FEEL LESS LIKE A SERVANT AND MORE LIKE A HOMESCHOOLING MOM. ALSO, BE FORGIVING OF YOURSELF. IF YOU DON'T HAVE A HOME THAT WOULD GRACE THE COVERS OF A MARTHA STEWART MAGAZINE BE THANKFUL. THAT MEANS YOUR HOUSE IS LIVED IN AND THE PEOPLE IN IT ARE PROBABLY MUCH HAPPIER TOO.

SCHEDULE ALL APPOINTMENTS (DOCTOR, DENTIST, ETC) ONE DAY A WEEK. ON THAT DAY, PLAN TO DO PARTICULAR ASSIGNMENTS, SUCH AS READING, THAT CAN BE DONE IN A WAITING ROOM OR VEHICLE.

TIME IS AN EARTHLY MEASURE. I SOMETIMES WORRY ABOUT IT FAR TOO MUCH. MY GOALS SHOULD BE IN THE ETERNAL REALM. WHEN I THINK OF ETERNITY, AND LIVE FOR THAT, I FIND THAT MY TIME ISSUES ARE OF MUCH LESS CONSEQUENCE. I WISH I COULD JUST KEEP THIS MINDSET WHEN I AM TRYING TO GET READY FOR CHURCH ON SUNDAY MORNING AND EVERYTHING IS GOING HAYWIRE! LOL

ROUTINES/SCHEDULES ARE NOT CHAINS TO BIND YOU; THEY ARE THE WINGS THAT HELP YOU FLY. USING A ROUTINE, MEANS THAT YOU CAN START AND STOP IT AS NECESSARY AND ISN'T TIME DEPENDENT. I HAVE HEARD BEFORE THAT YOU MAY THINK THAT YOU DON'T HAVE ROUTINES OR THAT YOU COULDN'T FOLLOW A ROUTINE; BUT YOU DO HAVE A ROUTINE, IT JUST DOESN'T HELP YOU IF IT IS A 'BROKEN' ROUTINE. CREATING A FEW ROUTINES FOR SPECIFIC TIMES OF DAY, MORNING, BEFORE BED, BEFORE HUSBAND COMES HOME, SCHOOL TIME, ETC., CAN REALLY HELP YOU MANAGE WHAT SEEMS TO BE UNMANAGEABLE.

PLANNING FREES UP DAILY LIFE. I SPEND A FEW WEEKS PLANNING BEFORE SCHOOL STARTS. THESE SAVES HOURS OF THINKING ON MY FEET/REACTING/WASTING TIME FIGURING THINGS OUT AND SIMPLIFIES OUR SCHOOL LIFE. SCHEDULE TIME FOR MOMMY EXERCISE AND 15 MINUTES ALONE TO THINK. IF IT'S NOT IN THE SCHEDULE IT WILL NEVER HAPPEN; IF IT'S SCHEDULED IT WILL HAPPEN ENOUGH TO MAKE A DIFFERENCE. FRANTIC MINDS LEAD TO FRANTIC LIFE/SCHOOL. TAKE TIME TO FIND CALM.

KEEP A SHOPPING LIST ON THE FRIDGE WHEN YOU RUN OUT OF THINGS YOU CAN ADD THEM TO THE LIST, THIS SAVES TIME WHEN YOU NEED TO MAKE UP THE LIST AND AT THE STORE.

LET OTHERS HELP.

KEEP A BOTTLE OF WINDEX, SCRUB FREE SINK CLEANER AND A ROLL OF PAPER TOWELS IN EACH BATHROOM. REQUEST THAT EACH FAMILY MEMBER CLEANS UP AFTER THEMSELVES BY WIPING UP MESSES AFTER THEIR TURN IN THE RESTROOM. THIS WILL KEEP YOUR RESTROOMS "COMPANY READY" LONGER AND LEAVING SUPPLIES IN EACH BATHROOM SAVES TIME.

KEEP A CALENDAR (ONE SMALL ENOUGH TO TAKE WITH YOU AND LARGE ENOUGH TO BE FUNCTIONAL) AND WRITE DOWN EVERYTHING THAT THAT COMES UP THAT YOU NEED TO DO. THIS KEEPS YOU ON TRACK AND ALSO SERVES AS A RECORD OF YOUR LIFE! SET "COMPUTER HOURS" OR "TEACHER PREP TIME" FOR YOURSELF AND STICK WITH IT.

I MAKE LISTS OF NEEDS FOR MYSELF AND FOR MY HUSBAND. I TALK TO OTHER FAMILIES FROM CHURCH ABOUT HOW THINGS GO AT THEIR HOUSES. I TRY TO PRIORITIZE SO IMPORTANT THINGS GET ACCOMPLISHED.

HAVE YOUR SHOWER AT NIGHT BEFORE YOU JUMP IN BED - THAT WAY YOU'RE ALWAYS CLEAN IN YOUR LOVELY BED, AND YOU DON'T HAVE TO WANDER ABOUT IN YOUR DRESSING GOWN IN THE MORNING TRYING TO FIT A SHOWER IN BEFORE SCHOOLING, YOU CAN JUST GET DRESSED 'CAUSE YOU'RE STILL CLEAN.

USE CHORE CHARTS THAT ARE COLOR CODED PER PERSON IN THE HOUSE.

A BASIC MENU PLAN WITH ONE MONTHLY LARGE TRIP TO THE GROCERY/MEGA STORE. THEN PICK UP MILK AND SUCH EACH WEEK.

WE MOVED OUR SCHOOLROOM INTO THE KITCHEN AREA INSTEAD OF HAVING IT IN A SEPARATE ROOM OF THE HOUSE. NOW I CAN WORK ON MY JOBS WHILE THE KIDS WORK ON THEIR SCHOOLWORK. THIS IS WAAAAAY MORE EFFICIENT!

WORKING TOGETHER AS A TEAM. LETTING EACH CHILD HAVE RESPONSIBILITIES AND TRAINING THEM TO DO A THOROUGH JOB. HAVE CERTAIN AREAS OF THE HOUSE THAT GET CLEANED ON SPECIFIC DAYS. DON'T TRY TO DO TOO MUCH IN ONE DAY. HAVE CHILDREN LEARN TIME MANAGEMENT AND GIVE THEM AN ALLOTTED TIME TO GET THE WORK DONE. MOMS, GET OFF THE COMPUTER!

HAVE A BASKET THAT EVERYTHING LAYING AROUND THE HOUSE GETS PUT IN. AT THE END OF THE DAY THE BASKET IS CLEANED OUT AND THINGS ARE PUT UP.

FORMS, FORMS, FORMS! WRITE IT DOWN AND THEN CHECK IT OFF AS IT GETS ACCOMPLISHED.

START LOOKING AT YOUR EVERYDAY ACTIVITIES, AND SEE HOW THAT CAN BE VIEWED AS EDUCATIONAL. MY DAUGHTER IS HELPING WITH THE COOKING AND BAKING, AND THAT COUNTS FOR HOME EC, AND SHE IS LEARNING ABOUT OTHER COUNTRIES AND FOOD, SHE USES MATH, READING, ETC. WE TALK ABOUT THINGS ALL THE TIME IN THE CAR...POLITICS, RELIGION, HISTORY. USING THE CAR AS AN EDUCATIONAL TOOL HAS BEEN A HUGE TIMESAVER FOR US. RATHER THAN WASTED TIME, IT HAS BECOME A MAIN STAPLE IN OUR HOMESCHOOLING DAY. WHEN IN TOWN WAITING FOR ANOTHER CHILD'S ACTIVITY, WE BRING ALONG SCHOOLWORK AND DO IT TOGETHER. IT IS A TIME WHEN THERE ARE FEWER INTERRUPTIONS, SUCH AS THE PHONE, ETC.

HAVE SCHOOL IN ITS OWN SPACE. IF YOU HOMESCHOOL ON THE KITCHEN TABLE, YOU HAVE TO PUT BOOKS AWAY TO EAT AND THEN GET THEM BACK OUT AFTER YOU'VE CLEANED UP FROM THE MEAL. IF YOU HAVE A SCHOOL TABLE IN ANOTHER LOCATION, BOOKS CAN BE LEFT OPEN WHERE THEY ARE, WHILE LUNCH AND CLEAN UP ARE TAKING PLACE.

A CHILD WHO IS OLD ENOUGH TO WALK AROUND IS OLD ENOUGH TO HELP MAINTAIN THE HOUSEHOLD. THIS REQUIRES SIGNIFICANT SUPERVISION AT FIRST, BUT LEADS TO A HUGE TIME SAVER VERY QUICKLY. WHILE THEY'RE HELPING CLEAN UP, SMALL CHILDREN AREN'T MAKING MESSES SOMEWHERE ELSE.

USING A TIMER... EVEN THE MOST DREADED TASK SEEMS MANAGEABLE IF YOU KNOW YOU ONLY HAVE TO GIVE IT YOUR BEST IT FOR 15 MINUTES! 99% OF THE TIME, THAT TASK WILL BE WELL COMPLETED BEFORE THE TIMER DINGS!!

#1 MY KIDS LOVE 5-10 MIN "PANIC CLEANING" WE'VE DONE IN THE PAST. AFTER AN HR OF WORKING HARD ON A SUBJECT, SET THE TIMER AND DO 5-10 MINS (DEPENDING ON THE SCHEDULE FOR THE DAY) OF CLEANING, TIDYING, OR WHATEVER. #2 MAKE IT A "SUBJECT" IN "LIFE SKILLS" CLASS. GET THE KIDS INVOLVED REGULARLY. #3 DON'T SWEAT THE DETAILS. SOMETIMES JUST GETTING THE CLUTTER PICKED UP AND THE OBVIOUS STUFF DONE IS ALL THERE'S TIME/ENERGY TO HANDLE. #4 CLEAN THE SHOWER WHILE YOU'RE IN IT... YOU'RE CLEANING YOURSELF, WHY NOT A SECTION OF THE WALL TOO? HAVE THE BOYS CLEAN THE BACK OF THE TOILET (THAT SPACE BETWEEN THE LID'S HINGES AND THE TANK) AFTER THEY USE IT THEMSELVES. WIPE DOWN THE SINK & COUNTER AS PART OF THE ROUTINE OF PUTTING THE STUFF YOU USE TO GET READY FOR THE DAY AWAY. #5 PUT IT BACK RIGHT AWAY! USE IT, THEN PUT IT AWAY.

WWW.FLYLADY.NET HAS HELPED ME TREMENDOUSLY. THE FLYLADY ENCOURAGES ROUTINES AND USING A TIMER. HER MOTTO IS "YOU CAN DO ANYTHING FOR 15 MINUTES." THAT HAS REALLY STUCK WITH ME AND MADE A HUGE DIFFERENCE IN MY LIFE.

BEING CONSISTENT WITH SMALL CHORES MEANS THAT I RARELY HAVE A LARGE MESS TO DEAL WITH.

PREPARE 2 CASSEROLES INSTEAD OF ONE WHEN PREPARING A MEAL. PUT THE SECOND IN THE FREEZER FOR FUTURE USE. GET CHORES DONE BEFORE YOU START SCHOOL, IT IS MUCH QUICKER THAN LETTING THE HOUSE GET A TOTAL WRECK.

I SPEND ALMOST ALL OF MY GROCERY MONEY IN ONE STORE--I MADE A LIST OF ITEMS THAT WE BUY AND PUT THE LIST IN THE SAME ORDER AS THE STORE'S ARRANGEMENT. THEN I PRINTED A COPY AND POSTED IT ON THE FRIDGE. ANYTIME SOMEONE REALIZED WE WERE OUT OF SOMETHING, THEY JUST CIRCLED THE ITEM ON THE LIST. WHEN IT WAS TIME TO GO GROCERY SHOPPING, MY LIST WAS ALREADY PREPARED, AND I COULD ZOOM IN AND OUT OF THE GROCERY STORE IN RECORD TIME, WITH NO BACKTRACKING ALL OVER THE STORE! THIS CUT MY GROCERY STORE TIME ABOUT IN HALF.

I ASSIGN ONE CHILD A DAY TO BE RESPONSIBLE FOR MAKING AND PASSING OUT A SIMPLE MORNING SNACK. THE PURPOSE OF THIS IS TWO-FOLD: FIRST, I AM NOT CONSTANTLY NAGGED BY CHILDREN WANTING SOMETHING TO EAT BECAUSE THEY KNOW WE HAVE A SET SNACK TIME(AND THEY'LL LOSE IT IF THEY ASK BEFORE IT'S SNACK TIME) SECOND, I CAN CONTINUE ON WITH SCHOOL WHILE ONE OF THE KIDS IS MAKING/GATHERING THE SNACKS.

I USED TO TRY TO GET THINGS DONE WHILE THE KIDS READ TO ME, BUT NOW I JUST TAKE THE TIME TO TOTALLY FOCUS ON THEM. IT IS FUNNY BUT I STILL GET EVERYTHING DONE AND DON'T FEEL AS FLUSTERED.

I DON'T FOLD SOCKS OR UNDERWEAR. WE HAVE A SOCK BOX AND ONLY BUY WHITE SOCKS. EASY TO REACH IN AND GRAB WHAT YOU NEED.

I HAVE THE 'WEEKLY' HOUSE CLEANING BROKEN DOWN INTO DAILY CHORES SO A LITTLE GETS DONE EVERY DAY RATHER THAN HAVE A MARATHON DAY:

1. INVEST IN A DIVIDED DIRTY CLOTHES HAMPER (OR BUY SEVERAL). AS EVERYONE GETS UNDRESSED AT NIGHT HAVE THEM PUT THEIR DIRTY CLOTHES IN THE APPROPRIATE HAMPER, I.E.; WHITES, DARKS, LIGHTS.

2. PUT A LOAD OF LAUNDRY IN THE WASHER AS SOON AS YOU GET UP IN THE MORNING.

3. HAVE EVERYONE PARTICIPATE IN FOLDING LAUNDRY WHILE YOU READ ALOUD OR WATCH TV.

4. HAVE A WEEKLY DINNER MENU PLANNED SO YOU KNOW WHAT TO BUY AT THE GROCERY STORE AND SO YOU'RE NOT IN A PANIC AT 5 P.M. TRYING TO DECIDE WHAT TO MAKE FOR DINNER.

5. PICK UP THE CLUTTER FROM YOUR HOME DAILY SO THINGS DON'T GET OUT OF HAND.

6. DON'T LET PILES OF ANYTHING GROW ANYWHERE IN YOUR HOME. THEY ARE TOO OVERWHELMING TO TACKLE.

WE COUNT EVERY OTHER FRIDAY AS HOME ECONOMICS DAY. WE USE THIS DAY TO CLEAN, SHOP, COOK, COMPLETE HOUSEHOLD PROJECTS, ETC. AND SOMETIMES AS A DAY TO CATCH UP ON INCOMPLETE WORK. THIS HAS HELPED REDUCE STRESS FOR ME AND MY CHILDREN.

OUR CHILDREN (AGES 5 AND 9) ARE PAID FOR THE HOUSEHOLD JOBS THAT THEY DO. THEY HAVE A LIST OF AGE/ABILITY APPROPRIATE JOBS THAT THEY CAN CHOOSE FROM, KNOW IN ADVANCE HOW MUCH THOSE JOBS PAY, TRACK THE JOBS THEY COMPLETE AND TURN IN THE JOB CHECKLIST AT THE END OF THE WEEK TO EARN THEIR "PAYCHECK". THEIR JOB CHECKLIST HELPS THEM CALCULATE AMOUNTS THAT GO TO GIVING, SAVING AND SPENDING. GETTING OUR CHILDREN INVOLVED IN KEEPING HOUSE TEACHES THEM PERSONAL RESPONSIBILITY, TEAMWORK, THE SATISFACTION OF EARNING AND SAVING MONEY AND THE JOY OF TITHING.

HAVE A LIBRARY BAG FOR COMPLETED BOOKS TO GO INTO- NO RUNNING AROUND TRYING TO FIND ALL THE LIBRARY BOOKS.

HAVE EVERYONE KEEP THEIR DESK AND/OR DRAWERS CLEAN. IT MAKES IT EASIER TO FIND WHAT YOU NEED QUICKLY. WE ALSO HAVE OUR SCHOOL SUPPLIES ORGANIZED: PENCILS ARE SHARPENED AND KEPT IN A LABELED BOX, COLORED PENCILS, MARKETS AND CRAYONS HAVE ANOTHER BOX, AND GLUE, TAPE AND VARIOUS ART SUPPLIES IN ANOTHER. KEEP A TIMER HANGING UP IN OUR CLASSROOM. THIS KEEPS LESSONS FROM BEING DRAWN OUT TOO LONG (ESPECIALLY THOSE THAT CHILDREN CAN GET CAUGHT UP IN). LAST, WE HAVE A CHORE CHART HANGING UP THAT REMINDS EVERYONE TO CLEAN UP THEIR DESK AREAS DAILY AND THEN A WEEK'S END CLEANING LIST: SHARPENING PENCILS, EMPTYING SHARPENER, CLEANING CHALKBOARD, WIPING DOWN DESK AND DUSTING THE BOOKCASES, GLOBE AND DRAWER UNITS. KEEP IT A TEAM EFFORT!

HAVING A MENU PLANNED OUT FOR THE WEEK OR TWO WEEKS. I LOVE KNOWING WHAT I NEED TO THAW THE NIGHT BEFORE AND WHAT I CAN PUT IN THE CROCK IN THE MORNING TO NOT HAVE TO WORRY ABOUT! I MAKE A GROCERY LIST AND BUY ONLY THE STUFF I NEED FOR THAT WEEK. ALSO, I TRY AND SAVE TIME IN THE MORNING BY MAKING BREAKFAST (OR PREPARING A BIG PORTION OF IT) AT NIGHT THE DAY BEFORE. COOKING AHEAD ON WEEKENDS HAS SAVED MY TIME DURING THE WEEK DAY TOO.

SCHEDULE THINGS LIKE PIANO LESSONS, SPORTS, ETC. ON THE SAME DAY IF POSSIBLE. THIS LIMITS THE AMOUNT OF TIME YOU ARE AWAY FROM HOME. THERE'S NOTHING WORSE THAN WASTING TIME DRIVING AROUND TOWN.

DEFINITELY, START WITH THE WORK, OR MORE DRUDGERY-ORIENTED TASK FIRST. IF THE KIDS HAVE A REWARD COMING AFTER THEIR SCHOOL WORK/CHORES ARE DONE, THEY ARE MORE MOTIVATED TO GET THEIR WORK DONE. SWIMMING, FOR INSTANCE. OR A VIDEO, SINCE BY THEN MOM IS EXHAUSTED ANYWAY.

I LOVE BLEACH WIPES! I KEEP ONE CONTAINER ON EVERY FLOOR OF MY HOUSE, SO I CAN WIPE SURFACES DOWN WHILE I AM THERE ON OTHER ERRANDS!

STAYING ON TASK. IF I AM DUSTING, AND I COME ACROSS SOMETHING THAT IS NOT WHERE IT SHOULD BE. IF I LEAVE TO PUT THAT ITEM BACK WHERE IT BELONGS, THEN I FIND SOMETHING IN THAT ROOM THAT NEEDS TO BE DONE, I WILL NEVER GET BACK TO DUSTING. I MAKE PILES IN THE ROOM THAT I AM IN. THINGS TO PUT BACK SOMEWHERE ELSE, TRASH, GIVE AWAY. THEN WHEN I AM DONE WITH THAT ROOM, I GO TO TAKE THE PILES AND DO WITH THEM AS NEEDED. THEN MOVE ON.

TRAIN THE CHILDREN TO DO THOSE THINGS THEY CAN (WHICH IS WAY MORE THAN MOST PEOPLE GIVE THEM CREDIT FOR BEING ABLE TO HANDLE). THIS DOUBLES AS LIFE SKILLS TRAINING FOR WHEN THEY LEAVE HOME.

Things that keep me from using
my time wisely:

Ideas to make our homeschool time more productive:

Time Savers and Ideas to try:

IDEAS TO HELP YOUR KIDS MANAGE THEIR TIME BETTER:

I WOULD SAY LESS TV OR VIDEO GAME TIME AND MORE TIME WITH EDUCATIONAL THINGS. THEY WILL LEARN LATER IN LIFE THAT VIDEO GAMES COME AND GO BUT KNOWLEDGE IS FOREVER PROVIDE THEM WITH A CHECK LIST OF THINGS TO GET DONE. AS THEY COMPLETE THE TASKS, SEEING THINGS GET CHECKED OFF WILL GIVE THEM A SENSE OF ACCOMPLISHMENT AND URGE THEM ALONG....

FREQUENT BREAKS (OUTSIDE IF POSSIBLE) TO EXPEND ENERGY.

DO THE BEST YOU CAN AND GIVE MOM A BREAK SHE'S LEARNING TOO.

DO YOUR SCHOOL WORK FIRST THEN YOU HAVE THE REST OF THE DAY TO DO OTHER THINGS.

DO YOUR WORK FIRST. GET AT IT AND GET IT DONE, THEN YOU HAVE ALL THE FREE TIME YOU WANT - AFTER THE WORK IS DONE.

PUT THEM TO BED KNOWING WHAT TOMORROW BRINGS. MAKE 3-7 ITEM LISTS FOR THEM TO BE RESPONSIBLE AS SOON AS THEY WAKE. DEPENDING ON UPPER OR LOWER GRADES, GIVE THEM YOUR GOAL FOR THE WEEK.

KEEP WORKING THROUGH A TASK UNTIL IT IS COMPLETED, BUT IF YOU MUST STOP WORKING ON SOMETHING BECAUSE YOU HAVE A QUESTION OR DON'T UNDERSTAND SOMETHING, WORK ON SOMETHING ELSE UNTIL YOU CAN GET BACK TO THE ORIGINAL WORK.

I USE A TIMER. I SET IT FOR THE AMT OF TIME IT SHOULD TAKE TO COMPLETE AN ASSIGNMENT. MOST OF THE TIME MY SON COMPLETES HIS WORK WITHIN THAT TIME FRAME. IF HE DOESN'T, IT'S MY CUE TO SEE IF HE IS STRUGGLING AND NEEDS ASSISTANCE OR IF HE'S JUST GOOFING OFF. WE'VE ENCOUNTERED BOTH.....CAN YOU IMAGINE THAT? :)

GIVE THEM OWNERSHIP OF THEIR DAY RATHER THAN THEM BEING SO DEPENDENT ON THE PARENT.

LET THEM KNOW WHAT'S EXPECTED OF THEM. HAVE A ROUTINE...DAILY... SO THEY CAN BE IN THE HABIT OF FOLLOWING A SCHEDULE.

THEY NEED TO KNOW WHAT TO DO. HOW TO GET STARTED. TEACH THEM TO BE MANAGERS OF THEIR TIME.

LET THEM KNOW THERE ARE CONSEQUENCES FOR DAWDLING. LIKE, WHEN IT'S FREE TIME IN THE AFTERNOON, THAT'S WHEN YOU GET TO DO THE CHORES, MATH, ETC. YOU SHOULD HAVE DONE EARLIER.

OBEY THE FIRST TIME. HAVE A GOOD ATTITUDE. RESPOND IN KIND, WHEN SPOKEN TO.

THIS HAS BEEN A DIFFICULT AREA FOR US. OUR KIDS ARE SO INVOLVED IN OUTSIDE ACTIVITIES, THAT WHEN THEY ARE HOME, THEY ARE WANTING TO JUST RELAX. WE ARE USING, WITH THE OLDER KIDS (TEENAGERS) A CONTRACT TYPE OF THING. THEY HAVE SO MUCH THEY ARE RESPONSIBLE FOR GETTING DONE IF THEY WANT TO DO THEIR OUTSIDE ACTIVITY THAT DAY. THE YOUNGER TWO HAVE MORE ONE-ON-ONE TIME.

USE YOUR TIME WISELY. IF YOU ARE WAITING WHILE OTHERS ARE BEING HELPED, WORK ON SOMETHING ELSE. IF YOU WAKE UP EARLY IN THE MORNING, GET STARTED ON YOUR WORK. DON'T WASTE TIME WAITING FOR SOMEONE TO SUGGEST THAT YOU DO SOMETHING. GET PLENTY OF REST. GIVE ALL DILIGENCE TO WHATEVER TASK IS SET BEFORE YOU.

REMEMBER THAT IT COULD BE WORSE ... WORKSHEETS INSTEAD OF GAMES, FOR EXAMPLE.

DO THE HARD STUFF FIRST, THEN COAST. START ON TIME SO YOU CAN GET DONE. ASK FOR WHAT YOU NEED, WITHOUT WAITING ON ANYONE TO FIGURE IT OUT. BE CREATIVE; SUGGEST ADDITIONAL OR ALTERNATIVE

IDEAS FOR GETTING A SCHOOLY-JOB DONE (E.G., "MAY WE PLAY MUGGINS SOMETIME THIS WEEK FOR MATH TIME?"

BEFORE YOU SIT AT THE TABLE OR DESK MAKE SURE YOU HAVE YOUR PENCILS SHARPENED AND EVERYTHING HANDY THAT YOU MIGHT NEED. THIS WAY YOU AREN'T SEARCHING FOR ANY OF YOUR SUPPLIES DURING A BIG PROJECT. ALSO, LISTEN TO YOUR MOM. SHE REALLY DOES HAVE YOUR BEST INTERESTS AT HEART.

ABSOLUTELY NO TV OR GAMES BEFORE SCHOOL WORK IS COMPLETED. WE ALSO PLAN ONE OR TWO BREAKS SO NO ONE GETS TOO FRUSTRATED.

FROM THE BEGINNING HAVE A SCHEDULE OF SOME KIND. EVEN IF IT IS AS SIMPLE AS ONCE YOU AWAKE IN THE MORNING YOU WILL DO THE FOLLOWING THINGS-----AND BE AT THE SCHOOL DESK BY X TIME FOR SCHOOL. BUT HAVE A SCHEDULE THAT GIVES THEM BOUNDARIES AND TASKS TO COMPLETE. ALSO, TO JUST GET WORK DONE SO THAT YOU CAN HAVE FREE TIME AND NOT HAVE THAT HANGING OVER YOUR HEAD ALL DAY.

FOR INDEPENDENT WORK, OLDER CHILDREN CAN USE A TIMER. SET A TIMER FOR 30 MINUTES. WHEN THE TIMER GOES OFF, SEE WHAT YOU HAVE ACCOMPLISHED IN THAT 30 MINUTES. MAKE IT A PERSONAL GOAL TO WORK MORE EFFICIENTLY THE NEXT DAY.

Time Management problems
we have in our homeschool:

Ideas for using our time better:

Mistakes to Watch out for:

"What was your biggest mistake in homeschooling your kids... and If you could do it over again, what would you change about how you have homeschooled in the past?"

That was the question we asked our homeschooling families, and we got some outstanding responses with tips and suggestions that are well worth considering by both newbie and veteran homeschoolers alike.

As you go through these, here is a caveat: There obviously isn't an ultimate "right way" to homeschool that fits everyone. This is reflected in the responses you will find in this collection. In fact, some of the thoughts expressed here turn out to be the direct opposite of the advice given by other moms. However, you will notice that a few very definite patterns will emerge as you read through these. So our suggestion to you is this: Do any of these speak to you in your situation? Are there lessons you can learn from the experiences of these other moms that can be applied to your own homeschooling?

Glean and learn... read through this with a highlighter or pencil in hand, and make your own observations, notes and comments as you go. There are some true golden nuggets just for you here, if you are willing to find them!

WE WOULD DO SOMETHING EVERY DAY NO MATTER HOW LITTLE AND NOT HAVE A BIG STRESS ATTACK ABOUT ALL THE "TIME" WE THINK NEEDS TO BE SPENT ON THE BOOK WORK

I WOULD GO BACK AND EXPEND THE SAME CREATIVITY I HOMESCHOOLED WITH WHEN MY KIDS WERE IN KINDERGARTEN THRU 5TH GRADE AND CARRY THAT INTO THE JUNIOR HIGH AND HIGH SCHOOL YEARS (THAT TEND TO BE MORE "SERIOUS" AND LESS CREATIVE). INDEPENDENT LEARNING IS GREAT, BUT CO-OPERATIVE LEARNING BUILDS MEMORIES AND BONDS RELATIONSHIPS! MY! HOW FAST THEY GROW! YOU CAN NEVER GO BACK AND RECOVER THOSE YEARS.

BE MORE CONSISTENT IN OUR SCHEDULES.

I WOULD HAVE START EARLIER AND BEEN MORE ORGANIZED.

I WOULDN'T WORRY SO MUCH ABOUT FORMAL SCHOOLING AND ACADEMICS IN PRESCHOOL, KINDERGARTEN AND GRADE ONE. THERE WOULD HAVE BEEN LESS (OR NO) WORKSHEETS AND MORE TIME TO HAVE FUN. I WOULD HAVE SPENT MORE TIME OUTDOORS AND GIVEN MY CHILD THE TOOLS WITH WHICH TO EXPLORE AND CREATE.

LESS 'CURRICULUM', MORE READING AND ENJOYING MY CHILDREN.

I WOULD DO MORE HANDS ON PROJECTS TO HELP MY CHILDREN GRASP WHAT I'M TEACHING.

I WOULDN'T WORRY SO MUCH AND ENJOY MUCH MORE THAN WE HAVE TO THIS POINT. I WOULD ALLOW OTHERS TO HELP ME A LOT MORE ALONG THE WAY AND ACCEPT SUPPORT OF OTHERS MORE FREELY. I WOULD DEFINITELY LEARN TO BE MORE ORGANIZED!

RELAX MORE ABOUT MY EXPECTATIONS AND HAVE MORE FUN WITH THE KIDS, REALIZING THAT LIFE IS FULL OF LEARNING.

I WISH THAT I LEARNED A LITTLE ABOUT ALL SORTS OF METHODS AND WAYS OF EDUCATION INSTEAD OF JUST ONE POPULAR METHOD OF THE TIME. I WISH THAT I HAD OF STARTED TO SEEK GOD FOR THE DIRECTION OF OUR HOMESCHOOL YEARS BEFORE I ACTUALLY DID.

I WOULD HAVE GOT MYSELF ORGANIZED EARLIER ON. THESE DAYS I FEEL LIKE I'M IN A CONSTANT STATE OF TRYING TO CATCH UP, ALTHOUGH I'M LEARNING ORGANIZATIONAL SKILLS. IF I'D DONE IT EARLIER, I MIGHT HAVE BEEN ABLE TO TEACH MY CHILDREN MORE EASILY...

I WOULD HAVE TAKEN NOTES WHILE READING ALL THE WONDERFUL HOMESCHOOL RESOURCE BOOKS RATHER THAN THINKING I WOULD REMEMBER IT ALL.

I WOULD LET MY KIDS KNOW WHAT IS PLANNED FOR THE DAY. I ALWAYS SEEM TO FORGET TO LET THEM KNOW THAT.

TO NOT HAVE STARTED SO MANY EXTRACURRICULAR ACTIVITIES OUTSIDE THE HOME. I LET OTHERS TALK ME INTO SO MANY FOR FEAR MY SON WOULDN'T HAVE A SOCIAL LIFE. WE ARE OVER COMMITTED AND ARE HAVING TO CUT BACK JUST TO GET THE BASIC SUBJECTS COVERED.

I THINK I WOULD NOT HAVE TAKEN MYSELF SO SERIOUSLY. THAT WOULD HAVE TAKEN SOME OF THE PRESSURE OFF THIS 'PERFECTIONISTIC' MOM AND MY 'LESS THAN PERFECT' CHILDREN! WE'RE STILL LEARNING TOGETHER AS A FAMILY AND WE'RE STILL TALKING TO EACH OTHER SO IT WAS REALLY WORTH EVERY MINUTE!

I WOULD HAVE BEEN MORE RELAXED WITH MY ELDEST DAUGHTER'S KINDERGARTEN YEAR. WE WOULDN'T HAVE USED A PRESCRIBED CURRICULUM. I WOULD HAVE TAUGHT HER THROUGH PLAY AND GAMES LIKE I HAVE THE NEXT 3 CHILDREN.

NOT TO OVER PLAN MY/THEIR SCHEDULE. I SEEM TO FALL IN THE TRAP OF TRYING TO MAKE SURE THEY EXPERIENCE EVERYTHING THEY WOULD NORMALLY EXPERIENCE IN TRADITIONAL SCHOOL. I JUST NEED TO LEARN TO RELAX!

I WOULD PLAY MORE WHILE THEY ARE YOUNG. I WOULD ALSO FOCUS ON TRAINING IN GOOD HABITS AND WAIT FOR THE ACADEMICS.

I WOULD GO BACK TO THE BEGINNING AND CHANGE THE WAY I WAS AS 'THE TEACHER'. I WOULD BE A MORE SCHEDULED AND QUICKER TO CHANGE THE CURRICULUM. I WOULD DO MORE FUN THINGS NOT JUST BOOKWORK.

WHEN WE FIRST STARTED HOMESCHOOLING OUR SON I SET IT UP LIKE A REGULAR SCHOOL. HE HAD TO READ AND DO EVERYTHING ON HIS OWN. (HE WAS IN 8TH GRADE!). I WOULD HAVE BEEN A LITTLE EASIER ON HIM AND ENJOYED JUST BEING WITH HIM AND HELPING HIM LEARN, NOT JUST MAKING HIM DO IT ON HIS OWN.

HAVING A DEDICATED SPACE THAT IS OUT OF THE MAIN TRAFFIC FLOW OF THE HOUSE, DEDICATED TO SCHOOLING!!

SOMEPLACE WE CAN SHUT THE DOOR & "GET AWAY FROM SCHOOL" WHEN WE ARE NOT "ACTIVELY" DOING OUR BOOK LESSONS. YOU NEED A DEDICATED SPACE, AND WE HAVE IT. WE JUST CAN'T SHUT THE DOOR AND "LEAVE IT".

RELAX DURING THE YOUNGER ELEMENTARY YEARS BY SPENDING MORE TIME READING AND OBSERVING NATURE AND LESS TIME DOING "SCHOOL WORK."

WE WASTED VALUABLE TIME WITH "UNSCHOOLING" PRACTICES. WHEN LEFT TO THEMSELVES, MOST CHILDREN DO NOT APPLY THEMSELVES AS THEY SHOULD. CHILDREN NEED GENTLE AND CONSISTENT PRODDING. MAKING UP GROUND LATER CAN BE VERY PAINFUL FOR ALL INVOLVED. 2. WE TRIED TO DO TOO MUCH OF THE CURRICULUM OURSELVES. WE WOULD HAVE INVESTED IN GOOD CURRICULUM EARLY ON (YOU NEED TO READ REVIEWS AND FIND WHAT IS EFFECTIVE AND COMPATIBLE WITH YOUR PHILOSOPHY OF EDUCATION.)

I LOVE HOMESCHOOLING. IF I COULD CHANGE SOMETHING, I WOULD HAVE MORE PATIENCE. THE LORD IS USING OUR HOMESCHOOLING JOURNEY TO HELP THAT DEPARTMENT!

WE HAVE ALREADY CHANGED THIS.... BUT I WOULD BE LESS INVOLVED IN SUPPORT GROUPS AND THEIR ACTIVITIES AND JUST CONCENTRATE MORE ON FINDING GOOD FRIENDSHIPS FOR CHILD AND MYSELF. SUPPORT GROUPS AND ACTIVITIES ARE FINE, PER SE, BUT TEND TO CREATE A LOT MORE RUNNING AROUND AND FRENZY THAN THEY ARE WORTH. I'VE ALSO NOTICED THE TENDENCY FOR GOSSIP AND BACKBITING AMONG THESE GROUPS, AS THEY ARE RUN PRIMARILY BY WOMEN. I'M SURE THAT THEY HAVE CAUSED SOME AMOUNT OF HURT FEELINGS AND NEGATIVE ATTITUDES FOR SOME PARENTS.

I WOULDN'T HAVE BURNED OUT MY FIRST CHILD ON A COMPLETE CURRICULUM PACKAGE AT AGE 6. HE WAS NOT ENJOYING SCHOOL BY THE END OF THAT YEAR AND NEITHER WAS I!

1. OUR OLDEST DAUGHTER WAS BORED WITH THE 7TH GRADE CURRICULUM, SO WE LET HER WORK FASTER, FINISHING JR. HIGH. WE DID HIGH SCHOOL IN 13 MONTHS. I WISH INSTEAD I WOULD HAVE EXPANDED THE CURRICULUM - ESPECIALLY THE SCIENCE AND HISTORY - TO INCLUDE PROJECTS WHICH WOULD HAVE INTERESTED HER.
2. OUR GIRLS HAVE TOLD US THAT THE WORST THING WE DID WAS TO HAVE THEM JOIN THE CHURCH CAMPUS SCHOOL FOR ELECTIVES; WE AGREE WITH THEM. NOW WE HAVE CLUBS. THE MOMS TEACH AND ARE ALWAYS PRESENT.

TRYING TO MAKE MY CHILDREN INTO LITTLE ME. I HAVE TRIED TO LIVE MY YOUTH AGAIN THROUGH THEM, IT DOESN'T WORK SO DON'T TRY IT.

I WOULD DELETE THE WHOLE FIRST YEAR. I USED A BOXED CURRICULUM AND TRIED TO SIGN UP MY BOYS FOR TOO MANY OUTSIDE ACTIVITIES INSTEAD OF FOCUSING ON BEING AT HOME AND BUILDING IMPORTANT RELATIONSHIPS. I AM THANKFUL THAT WE HAVE A REDEEMING HEAVENLY FATHER.

WELL, WE HAVE LEARNED FROM EVERYTHING WE HAVE BEEN THROUGH, BUT WE PROBABLY WOULD NOT HAVE PUSHED THE OLDER BOYS TO BE SO ACADEMICALLY INCLINED SO EARLY. WE WOULD HAVE GIVEN THEM MORE TIME TO MATURE AT THEIR OWN RATE OF GROWTH. WE WOULD HAVE CONCENTRATED MORE ON CHARACTER ISSUES DURING THAT TIME PERIOD INSTEAD OF STRESSING ACADEMICS SO MUCH.

HOMESCHOOLING IS A PROGRESSION AND MOST PEOPLE GO THROUGH THE SAME STEPS. SCHOOL AT HOME... DE-SCHOOLING... FINDING YOUR OWN WAY (UNSCHOOLING, ECLECTIC, ETC.) -- THIS ALL SEEMS NECESSARY... SO I WOULD NOT CHANGE ANYTHING. (WELL, MAYBE I WOULD TRY TO SPEND LESS MONEY - ESPECIALLY IN THE BEGINNING.)

TO "FOLLOW MY OWN INSTINCTS" ABOUT THE CURRICULUM THAT "I" ORIGINALLY CHOSE, AND NOT TAKE THE PATH OF "FOLLOWING" OTHERS IN THEIR CURRICULUM CHOICE, JUST BECAUSE IT WAS THE CURRICULUM RAGE OF THE DAY. "MY CHOICE" FOR "MY FAMILY" IS ALWAYS RIGHT, AND BEST FOR "US". :) I HOPE THAT OTHERS WILL HAVE THE COURAGE TO KNOW THIS FOR "THEIR HOMESCHOOL".

NOT TO START OUT SO RIGID, ESPECIALLY IF YOU ARE PULLING YOUR CHILD OUT OF A PUBLIC SCHOOL SETTING.

I'D WORRY LESS ABOUT GETTING BOOK WORK DONE EVERY DAY AND MAKE MORE OPPORTUNITIES TO LEARN THROUGH PLAY. I WILL NEVER REGRET THE ENJOYABLE TIMES, ONLY THAT THERE WEREN'T MORE OF THEM.

DON'T SET UNREALISTIC GOALS OR HAVE UNREALISTIC EXPECTATIONS. TAKE TIME TO GET TO KNOW YOUR CHILD AGAIN (IF THEY HAVE BEEN IN REGULAR SCHOOL LIKE MY DAUGHTER WAS). ALSO, I FELT GOD LEADING ME IN THIS DIRECTION LONG BEFORE I ACTUALLY TOOK HER OUT OF SCHOOL. I SHOULD HAVE OBEYED GOD RIGHT AWAY WHEN I FIRST BECAME AWARE OF HIS WILL FOR US. IT IS A CHALLENGE TO UNSCHOOL!

I WOULD NOT WASTE SO MUCH MONEY ON FANCY "EDUCATIONAL" TOYS AND COUNTING BLOCKS AND JUST GO WITH SIMPLE LEGOS, M&M'S, AND BEANS...REMEMBER, KIDS SPELL LOVE AS T-I-M-E SPENT WITH THEM!

I WOULDN'T SPEND SO MUCH MONEY ON DIFFERENT CURRICULUM. I WOULD FIND WHAT WORKS, STICK WITH IT, AND CONVINCE MYSELF THAT MY CHILDREN AREN'T GOING TO MISS OUT ON SOMETHING ELSE THAT'S OUT THERE.

ENJOYING THEM MORE, NOT GETTING CAUGHT UP IN THE TYRANNY OF THE URGENT. LETTING GO OF WHAT OTHER PEOPLE THINK. MAKING SURE THAT I HAD THEIR HEART AS OPPOSED TO OUTWARD OBEDIENCE.

I WOULD BE MORE PATIENT WITH MY ELDEST. SHE WAS SLOW TO READ AND I PUSHED HER MORE THAN I OUGHT TO HAVE. IT HURT OUR HOMESCHOOLING RELATIONSHIP.

I WOULD HAVE MORE FUN WITH HANDS ON PROJECTS. I HAVE OFTEN GOT TOO CAUGHT UP IN QUANTITY OF WORK FINISHED AND WE HAVE MISSED OUT ON QUALITY LEARNING TIME. LUCKILY I HAVE THREE MORE LITTLE ONES WHO HAVE NOT REACHED KINDERGARTEN AND I WILL DO THINGS DIFFERENTLY WITH THEM.

I'D SHUN THE CRITICISM OF MY PARENTS INSTEAD OF FEEDING INTO IT.

SAVORED THE MOMENTS MORE….I DIDN'T KNOW HOW FAST OUR 4 CHILDREN WOULD GROW-UP. AND…I THINK I COULD HAVE STARTED SOONER. WE PULLED OUR TWO OLDEST CHILDREN OUT OF SCHOOL WHEN OUR OLDEST WAS IN THIRD GRADE. LOOKING BACK, I WISH I WASN'T SO AFRAID TO START HOME SCHOOOLING.

ENJOY EACH DAY FOR WHAT IT BRINGS. I WISH I WOULD HAVE PUT THE WORKBOOKS AWAY SOONER AND LEFT THEM THERE, UNIT STUDIES HAVE ALWAYS BEEN THE VERY BEST WAY FOR OUR CHILDREN TO LEARN. UNIT STUDIES ALLOWED EACH CHILD EXPRESS THEMSELVES AND EXCEL AT THEIR OWN SPEED. I ALSO WOULD HAVE LET EACH CHILD HELP IN PICKING THEIR STUDIES AT THE BEGINNING OF THE YEAR, WHEN I DO THIS THEY SEEM TO WANT TO PICK IT UP MORE OFTEN.

WHEN I FIRST BEGAN HOMESCHOOLING I SCHEDULED MY CHILDREN WITH MANY ACTIVITIES OUT SIDE OF THE HOME.

WE ALWAYS FINISHED THE SCHOOL DAY, BUT SIMPLE AT HOME TIME WAS LACKING. I WAS STRESSED, AS WERE MY CHILDREN, TRYING TO GET THEM FROM ONE THING TO THE NEXT. I HAVE RECENTLY CUT OUT EVERYTHING BUT ONE ACTIVITY FOR EACH CHILD, AND AM LOVING THE FREE TIME!

IF I COULD CHANGE SOMETHING ABOUT THE PAST, WE WOULD SIMPLY HAVE HAD MORE FUN AND HIT THE BOOKS LESS WHEN THE KIDS WERE YOUNGER. SURE, YOU NEED TO GET THEM READING AND OTHER FUNDAMENTALS STARTED, BUT WHEN IT STARTS TO CREATE STRESS FOR EVERYONE, YOU HAVE DONE TOO MUCH! NOW WE ARE HAVING MORE FUN AND LESS STRESS AND THEY ARE MORE HAPPY AND LEARNING JUST THE SAME.

I WOULDN'T PROCRASTINATE SO MUCH. THE TIME HAS JUST FLOWN AWAY. "I'LL DO THAT WITH THE CHILDREN IN ONE MINUTE, (ONE HOUR, ONE DAY, ONE WEEK)", AND THE TIME IS GONE.

I WOULD TAKE MORE TIME TO JUST WORK ON MY RELATIONSHIP WITH MY DAUGHTERS, AND DO FUN THINGS WITH THEM IN THE EARLY GRADES, INSTEAD OF SO MANY WORKBOOK PAGES. I WOULD SMILE MORE AND BE LESS STRESSED AND JUST BE THANKFUL FOR THE TIME I WAS HAVING WITH THEM. I WOULD BE MORE ASSERTIVE WITH MY HUSBAND ABOUT NEEDING HELP IN THE EVENINGS SO I COULD GET A BREAK AND BE REFRESHED AND ABLE TO CONCENTRATE ON THE 'FULL-TIME JOB' OF HOMESCHOOLING DURING THE DAY - INSTEAD OF SQUEEZING IT INTO MY TO-DO LIST OF CHORES, AND EVERYTHING ELSE.

I WAS SO HARD ON MY FIRST TWO CHILDREN, I KILLED THEIR LOVE OF LEARNING AND MADE THEM TOO NERVOUS TO BE WRONG. I WAS YOUNG AND SAW MY KIDS ACHIEVEMENT LEVEL AS A REFLECTION ON ME. I WOULD HAVE RELAXED MORE, HAD MORE FUN GETTING TO KNOW THEM AND THEIR INTERESTS AND TEACH ON THAT.

I WOULD MAKE A PLAN. WITHOUT A PLAN YOU END UP MEANDERING ALL OVER. A BASIC OUTLINE AND TIMELINE FOR WHEN YOU WANT TO DO THINGS WILL KEEP YOU ON TRACK AND HELP YOU FINISH THINGS BY THE END OF THE YEAR. I ALSO WISH I WOULDN'T HAVE PURCHASED SO MANY MATERIALS. MY BOOKSHELVES ARE FULL OF UNUSED BOOKS. I WOULD HAVE USED THE LIBRARY MORE AND BORROWED MORE UNTIL I KNEW WHAT I LIKED.

NOT PLANNING AS MUCH OF A WORK LOAD AS I DID THE FIRST YEAR. I TRIED TO FIT EVERY AREA OF THE KEY-LEARNING AREAS IN AS A SEPARATE SUBJECT. IT WOULD HAVE EITHER TAKEN A TEN HOUR DAY OR COVERING EACH AREA ABOUT ONCE A MONTH. I SOON REALIZED THAT BY ONLY DOING ONE ACTIVITY WE ARE NATURALLY COVERING SEVERAL AREAS OF LEARNING AT ONCE. THREE YEARS IN AND LIFE IS MUCH SIMPLER NOW, WE HAVE GAINED BACK A LOT OF EXTRA TIME TOO.

THANKING MY SISTER-IN-LAW FOR HER WELL-INTENTIONED "TEACHER'S ADVICE" BUT TELLING HER THAT I HAVE RESEARCHED THE AREA OF LEARNING TO THE ENTH DEGREE AND FEEL CONFIDENT TO COME UP WITH MY OWN IDEAS.

THAT I KNOW HOW MY CHILDREN LEARN BEST AND IT'S DIFFERENT FOR EACH ONE.

I WOULDN'T WORRY ABOUT THE SMALL STUFF AND SPEND MORE TIME JUST ENJOYING THE JOURNEY OF WATCHING MY CHILDREN GROW UP AND MATURE INTO THEIR RELATIONSHIP WITH THE LORD. WE DIDN'T DO AS MUCH PAPER WORK AS I WOULD HAVE LIKED, BUT IF I HAD IT TO DO OVER AGAIN I WOULD TRUST GOD MORE. LOOKING AT THE WAY MY BOYS HAVE TURNED OUT HAS GIVEN ME MORE REASON TO TRUST MY INSTINCTS AS A HOME SCHOOLING MOM AND I AM CONTEMPLATING HOME SCHOOLING MY FOUR GRANDCHILDREN AS WELL.

FIRST OF ALL, I WOULDN'T STRESS SO MUCH OVER MY KIDS' LACK OF PERFORMANCE IN SOME AREAS. ESPECIALLY WHEN MY OLDEST DIDN'T READ UNTIL HE WAS NINE. AT 13, HE'S AN EXCELLENT AND AVID READER. SECONDLY, WHEN OUR FAMILY WENT THROUGH TIMES OF CHANGE, LIKE MOVING OR NEW BABIES, I WISH I'D JUST KEPT UP ON THE BASICS AND LEFT ALL THE FLUFF. IT WOULD HAVE BEEN LESS STRESSFUL AND THEY MIGHT HAVE LEARNED THEIR MATH FACTS BY NOW. LASTLY, WHENEVER I GOT OVER-COMMITTED TO OUTSIDE WORK, OUR HOMESCHOOLING SUFFERED AND NO ONE HAD MUCH FUN.

I WOULD HAVE STARTED HOMESCHOOLING SOONER. MY DAUGHTER WENT TO PUBLIC SCHOOLS FOR KINDERGARTEN AND 1/2 OF FIRST GRADE. HER KINDERGARTEN EXPERIENCE WAS GREAT, AND I WORKED CLOSELY WITH HER TEACHER BY VOLUNTEERING AT THE SCHOOL. BUT HER FIRST GRADE TEACHER LABELED HER FROM THE FIRST WEEK AS A PROBLEM CHILD, INSISTING THAT I GET HER ON MEDICATION FOR ADHD, SOMETHING SHE DOESN'T HAVE. SHE PUT MY DAUGHTER DOWN AND IT TOOK ALMOST TWO YEARS BEFORE MY DAUGHTER STARTED TO ENJOY LEARNING AGAIN. SHE HAS NO DESIRE TO RETURN TO PUBLIC SCHOOL.

STOP STRESSING ABOUT HOW MUCH WE GET DONE IN A YEAR. THERE IS NO HARD & FAST RULE THAT "MATH TEXTBOOK A" NEEDS TO BE FINISHED IN "X" AMOUNT OF TIME. THE BEAUTY OF HOMESCHOOLING IS THAT YOU CAN RELAX AND LET THE KIDS MOVE AT THEIR OWN PACE.

I WOULD HAVE TAKEN MY OWN ADVICE AND SPENT TIME WITH MY OLDEST WHO IS NOW 19 YRS. OLD INSTEAD OF LEAVING HIM TO LEARN ON HIS OWN. I SHOULD HAVE MONITORED HIS WORK CLOSER RATHER THEN TRYING TO GIVE HIM THE RESPONSIBILITY FOR HIS OWN EDUCATION. BIG MISTAKE!

I WOULD HAVE BEEN SLOWER TO SPEND BIG MONEY ON CURRICULUM UNTIL I KNEW IT WAS GOING TO BE APPEALING AND EFFECTIVE WITH MY PARTICULAR CHILDREN'S LEARNING STYLE AS WELL AS MY OWN TEACHING STYLE.

I WOULD BE CONSISTENT. I DON'T THINK THE CURRICULUM MATTERS AS MUCH AS BEING CONSISTENT WITH WHAT YOU HAVE CHOSEN TO DO. A COMPLETED REGULAR TIME OF 15 MINUTES IS BETTER THAN A HOPED FOR 1 HOUR SESSION.

I WOULD NOT FORCE-TEACH A SKILL WHEN IT WAS CLEARLY STRAINING. I HAVE LEARNED THAT IF I WAIT FOR MORE SIGNS OF READINESS, OR PRESENT IT IN VERY SMALL AND UNIMPOSING WAYS, THERE IS AN "I CAN" ATTITUDE AND AMBITIOUS SPIRIT THAT COMES ALONG AND TAKES A CHILD MUCH MUCH FARTHER.

RELAX. DON'T FEEL THE PRESSURE TO BE SCHOOLY. OFTEN I DID THIS BECAUSE THAT IS THE SYSTEM I CAME OUT OF. IT TOOK A FEW MONTHS OF CONSTANTLY REMINDING MYSELF - THIS IS NOT A SCHOOL AT HOME. THIS IS LIFE SKILLS TRAINING AND THE READING, WRITING, AND MATHS WILL HAPPEN BUT NOT ACCORDING TO A RIGID EXTERNAL INSTITUTION'S TIMETABLE.

I WOULD BE OBEDIENT TO GOD'S CALL TO HOMESCHOOL EARLIER AND NOT HAVE PUT IT OFF UNTIL AFTER WE "TRIED" PUBLIC SCHOOL. EVEN THOUGH OUR PUBLIC SCHOOL EXPERIENCE WAS ONLY AT THE KINDERGARTEN LEVEL, IT STILL LEFT US WITH A LOT TO "UNDO" IN THE WAY OF SOCIAL AND ATTITUDE TRAINING. WE ARE STILL WORKING ON SOME OF THE BAD ATTITUDES (FOR EXAMPLE, "EVERYONE HATES MATH, AND SO DO I!") THAT HAS EVEN CARRIED OVER IN TO THE THIRD GRADE.

I PUSHED MY SON TO LEARN THE ALPHABET WHEN HE WAS ONLY 4, HE WOULD CRY WHEN I PULLED OUT THE FLASH CARDS. HE WOULD NEVER SIT WITH ME WHEN WE READ STORIES OR TRY TO READ ALONG IN THE BOOK. I HAD HIS EYES TESTED BUT THERE SEEMED TO BE NO PROBLEMS THERE, 3 YEARS LATER HE STILL COULDN'T/WOULDN'T READ. I ALMOST GAVE UP, BUT FORMAL TESTING FROM A CHILDREN'S SPECIALIST FOUND THE PROBLEM. WITH THE CORRECT GLASSES AND A CHANGE IN OUR TEACHING METHODS, HE HAS MADE UP ALMOST ALL OF HIS LOST GROUND. IF I HAD IT ALL TO DO AGAIN, I WOULD TRUST MY OWN INSTINCTS AND NOT LET OTHER SECOND GUESS ME :o(

I WOULD BE LESS PRESSURING OF MY OLDEST CHILD. I WOULD HAVE TAKEN IT SLOWER AND LET US BOTH APPRECIATE HIM BEING A LITTLE KID LONGER. I WOULDN'T HAVE RUSHED HIM INTO ELEMENTARY WORK IN KINDERGARTEN. I WOULD HAVE ENJOYED HIM MORE AND ACCEPTED AND MET HIM WHERE HE WAS. NOT THAT I DIDN'T DO THESE THINGS AT ALL, I JUST WOULD HAVE DONE THEM MORE, AND WORRIED LESS ABOUT GAPS IN THE EDUCATION. THEY HAVE A WAY OF FILLING IN OVER TIME.

DEAL WITH DISCIPLINE AT A EARLY AGE BECAUSE LITTLE PROBLEMS JUST BECOME BIGGER.

START OUT FINDING A CURRICULUM IN LANGUAGE ART AND MATH THAT YOUR CHILD ENJOYS AND STICK WITH IT THROUGHOUT... THIS WILL AVOID GAPS IN SCOPE AND SEQUENCE AND HELP THEM AVOID FRUSTRATION IN OTHER TEXTS DUE TO NOT HAVING COVERED CERTAIN AREAS YET. ALSO AS THE TEACHER, TAKE BREAKS FROM YOUR CHILDREN ONCE OR TWICE A MONTH. ALTHOUGH YOU LOVE YOUR CHILDREN DEARLY, SPENDING 24 HOURS PER DAY WITH THEM FOR MONTHS ON END WILL CAUSE PARENT AND CHILD TO TAKE THE OTHER FOR GRANTED AND NEVER GIVE THE OPPORTUNITY FOR APPRECIATING OUR JOURNEY TOGETHER.

I NOW HAVE A SITTER COME IN ONCE A WEEK TO STAY WITH MY CHILDREN. I DID NOT DO THAT BEFORE THIS YEAR. I WOULD HAVE DONE THAT FROM THE BEGINNING IF I HAD KNOWN HOW HELPFUL IT WOULD BE! I FEW HOURS AWAY TO RUN ERRANDS ALONE OR MEET WITH A FRIEND MAKES A BIG DIFFERENCE.

I WOULD CONCENTRATE MORE ON A HOME "EDUCATION" AND LESS ON A HOME "SCHOOL." AT FIRST I TRIED TO REPRODUCE A CLASSROOM AT HOME. THAT WAS A MISTAKE. EDUCATION HAS NOTHING TO DO WITH A CLASSROOM AND EVERYTHING TO DO WITH THE HEART AND MIND.

I WOULD TAKE THE TIME OFF WHEN I TOOK THEM OUT OF PUBLIC SCHOOL. I DIDN'T DO IT EVEN THOUGHT IT WAS SUGGESTED TO ME. I ENDED UP DOING IT LATER, BUT IT WORKED OUT OKAY IN THE END.

THE FIRST YEAR THAT I HOMESCHOOLED, I RECREATED SCHOOL AT HOME WITH BULLETIN BOARDS, DESKS, TIMERS (FOR BELLS), AND ALL SORTS OF THINGS THAT I THOUGHT THAT THEY WOULD SEE IN "REAL SCHOOL." I TOOK THE FUN AND COMFORT OUT OF HOMESCHOOL AND IT HAS BEEN DIFFICULT TO GET US ALL COMFORTABLE AGAIN. THANKFULLY, EVERY YEAR IT GETS BETTER.

I WOULD HAVE FOUND BENCHMARKS FOR BOTH OF MY CHILDREN SO I COULD MEASURE OUR SUCCESSES MORE EASILY.

THIS YEAR I'VE DONE THAT, AND I REALIZED THE PROGRESS WE'D MADE IN THE FIRST 12 WEEKS OF SCHOOL - MUCH MORE THAN I'D "FELT" LIKE WE'D MADE.

AT THE BEGINNING I TRIED TO FIT OUR HOMESCHOOLING DAY INTO CHUNKS OF TIME, SO THAT EACH SUBJECT HAD TO BE DONE DURING A CERTAIN TIME PERIOD. THIS LEFT ME FRUSTRATED AND DISAPPOINTED. NOW I HAVE A MORE RELAXED SCHEDULE, WHICH WORKS MUCH BETTER FOR ALL OF US.

I WOULD HAVE ENCOURAGED MY OLDER CHILDREN TO BE MORE INVOLVED IN TEACHING/HELPING THEIR SIBLINGS. THEY ALL WORK VERY WELL INDEPENDENTLY, BUT I WOULD LOVE TO SEE THEM EVEN READING TOGETHER MORE. THE LITTLE ONES LEARN SO MUCH FROM THE BIG ONES, BUT IT DOES NOT HAPPEN ENOUGH IN MY OPINION.

GET MORE AUDIO BOOKS SINCE I THINK IT'S GOOD FOR THE KIDS TO LEARN TO LISTEN AND I DON'T HAVE TIME OR THE VOICE TO READ 2-3 HRS A DAY.

BE FLEXIBLE TO THE EVER CHANGING NEEDS OF YOUR KIDS AND HOW THAT BLENDS WITH YOUR NEEDS AND ABILITIES, AND NOT FOLLOW THE "I'LL NEVER DO THAT". WHEN IT COMES TO HOMESCHOOLING, ONE NEVER KNOWS WHAT THE NEXT DAY WILL BRING IF YOU ARE WATCHING AND LISTENING.

I WOULD DEFINITELY LOOSEN UP MORE AND HAVE MORE FUN...SPEND MORE DAYS OUTSIDE PLAYING, OBSERVING NATURE, DOING ARTS AND CRAFT PROJECTS, DRAWING, PURSUING MY DAUGHTER'S INTERESTS.

NOT SPEND SO MUCH MONEY ON A BUNCH OF DIFFERENT STUFF! OVER THE YEARS I'VE LEARNED THAT LESS IS BEST AND I'VE STARTED GETTING RID OF SO MUCH JUNK. YOU CAN HAVE SO MUCH STUFF (WORKBOOKS, MAPS, MANIPULATIVES, ETC.) THAT YOU CAN'T EVEN FIND WHAT YOU REALLY NEED! AND THEN IT STRESSES YOU OUT BECAUSE YOU'RE BUYING IT AND NOT USING IT. KEEP IT SIMPLE SWEETIE!

SYSTEMATICALLY TEACH THE MULTIPLICATION TABLES, TEACH A PROPER WAY TO HOLD A PENCIL WHEN HANDWRITING, FIND A WAY TO HAVE REGULAR FAMILY DEVOTIONS OR BIBLE STUDY.

I WOULD HAVE READ MORE TO MY CHILDREN. READ, READ, READ! MY HUSBAND IS EXTREMELY SUPPORTIVE OF HOME EDUCATION, BUT HE WISHES HE HAD BEEN MORE INVOLVED IN A HANDS-ON WAY FROM THE BEGINNING.

WHEN WE STARTED, MY DAUGHTER WAS 4 1/2 - I WAS BUSTING, PREPARED AND READY TO BEGIN FORMAL SCHOOLING... .SHE WAS NOT. THE POOR LITTLE GIRL COMPLETED STACKS OF WORKBOOKS AND WORKSHEETS AND BEING 'FORCED' INTO THE LEARN-TO-READ LESSONS, BUT SHE WOULD HAVE BEEN SO MUCH BETTER OFF IF WE SPENT THE TIME READING STORIES, DOING NATURE WALKS AND DOING SCIENCE EXPERIMENTS.

I WOULD HAVE FINE-TUNED OUR HIGH SCHOOL CURRICULUM FROM THE OUTSET TO THE INDIVIDUAL NEEDS OF EACH STUDENT INSTEAD OF STICKING SO MUCH WITH THE TRADITIONAL WORKBOOK/TEXTBOOK METHOD. THERE WOULD HAVE BEEN MORE EMPHASIS EARLIER ON CREATIVE WRITING SKILLS.

IF I COULD DO IT ALL OVER, I NEVER WOULD HAVE SENT MY CHILDREN TO PUBLIC SCHOOL. I AM HAVING TO REVIEW AND REVISIT SO MANY TOPICS THAT I FEEL THAT I AM SPINNING MY WHEELS WHILE I AM RETEACHING CONCEPTS THAT THEY SHOULD HAVE ALREADY HAD A GRASP OF. ADDITIONALLY, I WOULD TAKE SOME TIME OFF TO LET MY KIDS DECOMPRESS FROM THE SCHOOL EXPERIENCE. THE FIRST COUPLE OF WEEKS WERE A REAL STRUGGLE BECAUSE THEY WERE STILL STRESSED ABOUT THE TRANSITION FROM SCHOOL TO HOME.

DISCOVER MY CHILD'S LEARNING STYLE. NOT RUN MY "SCHOOL" LIKE A GOVERNMENT SCHOOL. I WOULD HAVE LISTENED TO GOD'S VOICE AND STAYED HOME (NOT WORKED) WHEN MY CHILDREN WERE LITTLE AND HOMESCHOOLED RIGHT FROM THE START. BLESS GOD I LISTENED BEFORE IT WAS TOO LATE.

I WOULD HAVE TAKEN THE TIME TO TEACH MY FIRST COUPLE CHILDREN PROPER PENCIL TECHNIQUES AND LETTER FORMATION...I DIDN'T WANT TO STUNT THEIR CREATIVITY BY SHOWING THEM HOW, SO THEY DEVELOPED BAD HABITS THAT THEY NEVER WERE ABLE TO BREAK.

NOW THAT OUR OLDEST HAS JUST ENTERED COLLEGE, I WOULD GO BACK AND ENJOY HER LITTLENESS MORE, AND MAKE SURE WE DISCUSSED HER READINGS MORE COMPLETELY, AND GET TO THE DISCUSSIONS WE NEVER GOT AROUND TO DOING.

SPENT MORE TIME READING ALOUD, LESS GIVING LESSONS. LET THEM LEARN THINGS SUCH AS SPELLING AND WRITING BY JUST COPYWORK WRITING IN JOURNALS OR WHATEVER THEY WANT, ESP. AT A YOUNG AGE. SAVE ANYTHING THAT REQUIRES A TEACHER (SUCH AS FOREIGN LANGUAGE) FOR AGES 11+ WHEN THEY CAN TEACH THEMSELVES.

PROBABLY WORRY LESS ABOUT TRYING TO MATCH WHAT WE THOUGHT THE SCHOOLS WERE TEACHING AND CONCENTRATE ON A REAL EDUCATION. WHEN WE MET OTHERS WITH CHILDREN IN SCHOOLS (POOR THINGS!) WE FOUND THEY LEARNED FAR LESS THAN WE HAD SUPPOSED.

WHEN WE DECIDED TO HOMESCHOOL, WHEN WE KNEW IT WAS GOD'S WILL FOR OUR FAMILY...WE SHOULD HAVE BEGUN RIGHT THEN...THE BEST TIME TO BEGIN HOMESCHOOLING IS THE MOMENT YOU COME UNDER CONVICTION!

DON'T WAIT FOR THE "RIGHT TIME" TO PULL THEM OUT OF SCHOOL. NOW IS THE "RIGHT TIME"! ALSO, TO KEEP HOMESCHOOLING AS SIMPLE AND COST EFFECTIVE AS POSSIBLE. KEEPING IT SIMPLE.

I'D HAVE POLITELY LISTENED TO THE NAY-SAYERS AND THEN FORGOTTEN THEM COMPLETELY....INSTEAD OF LETTING THEM PLANT SEEDS OF SELF-DOUBT IN MY MIND! I'D ALSO HAVE BOUGHT A LOT LESS CURRICULUM, LOL. YOU DON'T NEED EVERY CURRICULUM ON SPELLING, OR PHONICS, OR WHATEVER. GO TO A LARGE HOMESCHOOL CONVENTION AND FORGET THE SPEAKERS, HEAD FOR THE VENDOR HALL AND SPEND ALL DAY HANDLING THE ACTUAL CURRICULUMS AND SITTING ON THE FLOOR READING THROUGH THEM. THEN MAKE A LIST OF THOSE THAT YOU LIKED AND GET ONLINE AT HOMESCHOOL FORUMS AND CHAT WITH OTHERS WHO ARE ALREADY USING THOSE AND THROUGH LOTS OF QUESTIONS AND DISCUSSION DECIDE WHICH MIGHT BE BEST FOR YOUR CHILD'S WAY OF LEARNING (THERE ARE PLENTY OF BOOKS ON THIS TOO).

I WOULD LIGHTEN UP DURING THE KINDERGARTEN AND FIRST GRADE YEARS IF I COULD DO IT OVER AGAIN. I WOULD MAKE SCHOOL MORE FUN AND DO FIELD TRIPS AND ART PROJECTS MUCH MORE OFTEN. I WAS SUCH A NEW HSER AND SOOO WORRIED ABOUT "DOING IT RIGHT - DOING REAL SCHOOL" THAT I WAS FAR TO UPTIGHT! SCHOOL GETS SERIOUS ENOUGH IN LATER YEARS.

I WOULD READ ALOUD TO MY SONS MORE, AND ENJOY THEM EXACTLY WHERE THEY'RE AT, THEY TRULY DO GROW UP SO QUICKLY. ALSO, I WOULD START EACH DAY WITH A QUIET TIME WITH THE LORD, ASKING HIM TO DIRECT OUR DAY--THIS ONE THING CAN MAKE ALL THE DIFFERENCE IN THE WORLD!

NOT TO TRY TO TEACH A PRESCHOOLER EVERY SUBJECT KNOWN TO MAN. I WAS JUST SO EXCITED ABOUT HOMESCHOOLING AND THERE WERE SO MANY WONDERFUL THINGS I WANTED TO SHARE WITH MY SON, THAT I TRIED TO FIT IN EVERY SUBJECT, EVERY WEEK. BIG MISTAKE.

I WOULD RELAX MORE AND ENJOY THE PROCESS. TEACHING A CHILD ISN'T LIKE AIMING A FIRE HOSE OF KNOWLEDGE AT THEM AND EXPECTING THEM TO DRINK FROM IT. IT IS MORE ABOUT FORMING RELATIONSHIPS AND CONNECTIONS EVEN IF THEY AREN'T READING OR PERFORMING AT GRADE LEVEL. IT IS MORE IMPORTANT TO JUST HANDLE THE SUBJECT MATTER AT THE CHILD'S PACE.

I'D BE MORE CONSISTENT IN REQUIRING OBEDIENCE THE FIRST TIME, AND NOT LET WHAT OTHERS THINK AFFECT ME MORE THAN WHAT THE LORD THINKS OF ME. I'D ALSO HAVE WASTED LESS TIME WITH THE SEEMINGLY "HARMLESS" ACTIVITIES AND SPENT MORE TIME ON THE THINGS THAT WILL MATTER IN ETERNITY.

IF I COULD CHANGE ONE THING, I WOULD NOT MAKE ACADEMIC DEMANDS AS EARLY AS I DID. I WOULD RECOMMEND THE BOOK "BETTER LATE THAN EARLY" BY DOROTHY AND RAYMOND MOORE, WHICH SUGGESTS THAT CHILDREN YOUNGER THAN 9 OR 10 (ESPECIALLY BOYS, AND I HAVE ONLY BOYS!) NOT BE REQUIRED TO DO SIT-DOWN ACADEMIC WORK. I INSISTED THAT MY TWO OLDER BOYS MEET CERTAIN ACADEMIC GOALS WHEN THEY WERE YOUNG, AND DEFINITELY NOT READY. NOW MY YOUNGEST SON, WHO I HAVE NOT MADE SIT DOWN AND DO ACADEMIC WORK, ACCOMPLISHES AS MUCH AND MORE IN HIS OWN WAY AT HIS OWN TIME.

I AM A VERY LAID BACK MOM WHEN IT COMES TO HOMESCHOOLING, WE DON'T HAVE A SET SCHEDULE AND ITS REALLY EASY FOR ME TO LET SCHOOLING SLIDE BY. IT HAS CAUSED US TO GET BEHIND IN HOMESCHOOLING AND I AM NOT HAPPY ABOUT THAT. I THINK HAVING A SCHEDULE AND BEING ABLE TO STICK TO IT REALLY HELPS I FOCUSED THE FIRST 2 YEARS ON A RIGID SCHOOL TIME AND I MISSED OUT ON GETTING TO KNOW MY SONS BETTER AFTER PULLING THEM OUT OF THE PUBLIC SCHOOL SYSTEM.

In what areas does our homeschool need to be changed?

Potential problems that need attention:

Things I personally need to work on:

I need some help with:

Friends and Resources we could tap into that would help our homeschool:

Summer Learning Ideas:

Don't take the entire summer off of everything. It can be a great time to try something new on a limited basis to see if it will fit with your family.

Don't force it. Make it fun. Enjoy each and every new discovery.

Cut the regular day in half, or at least do a little reading, writing and math, when ever dad is working, young siblings are napping or so you do not have to re teach months of work in the fall.

Plan for the next school year early, order curriculums early - worst thing is to start the year without materials.

Plan for a 32 week year instead of 38, in case an emergency comes up, you won't feel like you're behind.

Start slow. If you're kids are used to a long summer break, break long enough for them to get "bored" and then start up again. When it is time for the "new school year" have a "back to school" party to switch gears.

Relax, have fun, don't try to do too much, just enjoy your family time together. Drill math facts over summer and make reading books a priority!!

FIND CREATIVE WAYS TO INTEGRATE LEARNING. IT PAYS TO 'KEEP AT IT' (ALBEIT INFORMALLY), SO THAT VERY LITTLE - IF ANYTHING - FALL THROUGH THE CRACKS.

GET READY FOR NEXT "SCHOOL YEAR" BEFORE AUGUST. FORMAL LESSONS WILL SNEAK UP ON YOU SOONER THAN YOU THINK!!

HAVE A 'GRADUATION' CEREMONY WITH CERTIFICATES OF COMPLETION AND A PARTY! :) YOU DID IT! NOTE EVERYONE'S COMMENTS ON THEIR PAST YEAR WENT -- HIGHS & LOWS. TAKE INDIVIDUAL PHOTOS & A GROUP SHOT. MAKE A PLAN THAT FITS YOUR FAMILY - DON'T JUST DO WHAT THE PUBLIC SCHOOLS DO

HAVE LEARNING AS A LIFESTYLE, AND THERE'S NO NEED FOR A SUMMER BREAK. THERE ARE LEARNING OPPORTUNITIES ALL AROUND.

THIS IS A GOOD TIME TO DO ALL THE PROJECTS OR ACTIVITIES THAT YOU NEVER SEEM TO HAVE TIME FOR DURING THE NORMAL SCHOOL SCHEDULE. PROJECTS WE WORK ON ARE LEARNING NEW CHORES, ART AND CRAFT PROJECTS, HISTORY OR SCIENCE PROJECTS THAT REVIEW WHAT WE STUDIED THIS YEAR OR WERE OF INTEREST, BUT DID NOT FIT WITH WHAT WE STUDYING. ALSO GREAT TIME TO CATCH UP ON WRITING FRIENDS AND FAMILY THAT DO NOT LIVE CLOSE BY.

RELAX, EVERYTHING CAN COUNT AS HOMESCHOOLING, SO LONG AS YOU ARE ACTUALLY TALKING WITH YOUR CHILDREN. KEEP THE KIDS AWARE THAT LEARNING IS IN EVERY DAY THINGS. NOT JUST NOTEBOOKS AND WORKSHEETS.

IF YOUR CHILDREN HAVE BEEN STRUGGLING IN A SUBJECT REQUIRE SOMETHING EACH DAY. ONE LINE OF CURSIVE, ONE PAGE OF MATH, THREE PAGES OF A CHAPTER BOOK (OR A CHAPTER), UNTIL IT HAS COMPILED INTO AN HOUR OF WORK. WHEN WORK IS DONE THEY ARE FREE TO PLAY.

Do lots of museums, be outside as a family, do lots of cooking and science, rent movies that matched your studies, and get together with friends as much as possible.

A good time to find what interests your child and pursue them together. Also the perfect time to seek the Lord together and find creative ways of using their talents to be fruitful.

Have a plan on when you will 'start back' and have a clear idea of what you will do. I try to plan at the beginning of our break so that I can really relax, otherwise it is spinning in my head during our holiday.

Realize that it might take 2 weeks to get back into routine after the break. Plan for that! I find little incentives for those first 2 weeks help - a small treat for a good attitude.

Don't let the kids know that they are learning during the "fun activities". Enjoy the free time together and just have fun. You know that they are learning. ;)

Don't stop the math; keep working on it at least twice a week. Don't stop at all if you can "get away with it", instead plan 2 week breaks through out the year.....Truly plan them and do something completely different.....Travel, home repair, campout in the backyard, etc.

Have everyone keep reading! Most libraries have a summer reading program to encourage this so make use of it. Take the opportunity to make trips that you don't feel you have the time for during the school year. This can even be the local trips around town to see how businesses work.

DON'T NECESSARILY TRY TO WORK AHEAD, TRY NOT TO PLAY CATCH UP- JUST PUT THE BOOKS AWAY AND TAKE A BREAK, HOWEVER JUST KEEP READING SNUGGLE TIME.

MAKE A SUMMER SCRAPBOOK OF ALL THE FUN YOU HAVE. BUY EACH OF THE KIDS A CHEAP SCRAPBOOK AND DISPOSABLE CAMERA. SPECIAL SUMMER THEMED STICKERS CAN ALSO BE FUN. YOU CAN GO THROUGH MAGAZINES AND CUT OUT PICTURE TO ADD TO THE SCRAPBOOK. I WOULD PLAN AN ACTIVITY FOR THE WEEK SUCH AS GOING TO THE POND AND FEEDING THE DUCKS, AND THEN AN ARTS AND CRAFTS PROJECT RELATED TO OUR ACTIVITY FOR THE NEXT DAY SUCH AS COLORING A PICTURE OF A DUCK OR USING CONSTRUCTION PAPER TO CUT OUT THE SHAPE OF A DUCK. I WOULD CHECK OUT SOME BOOKS FROM THE LIBRARY TO READ ABOUT DUCKS FICTION AND NON-FICTION MAYBE EVEN A MOVIE. WE WOULD SPEND A DAY PUTTING EVERYTHING INTO OUR SCRAPBOOK FOR THE WEEK AND WRITING OUR JOURNAL ENTRY. AS YOU GO ABOUT YOUR SUMMER TAKE PICTURE OF YOUR ACTIVITIES AND COLLECT SOUVENIRS OF PLACES YOU VISIT OR THINGS YOU DO. FOR INSTANCE IF YOU PLANT A GARDEN TAKE PICTURES OF THE PROJECT AND THEN DRY LEAVES OR FLOWERS TO ADD TO THE SCRAPBOOK. IF YOU GO TO THE BEACH YOU CAN PUT A SHELL OR A SMALL BAGGIE OF SAND TO ADD TO YOUR BOOK. IF YOU GO TO THE MOVIES SAVE YOUR TICKET STUB.   MAKE YOUR SCRAPBOOK A TWO PAGE SPREAD STYLE BY ADDING PICTURES, CRAFTS AND SOUVENIRS TO THE FIRST PAGE AND ON THE SECOND HAVE THE CHILD JOURNAL ABOUT WHAT THEY DID.

DO ARTS AND CRAFTS PROJECTS SMALL ENOUGH TO FIT INTO THE SCRAPBOOK. GET SOME DRAWING BOOKS FROM THE LIBRARY ABOUT BIRDS AND PRACTICE DRAWING AND ADD THE SMALL DRAWINGS TO THE SCRAPBOOK ON THE DAY YOU WENT BIRDING IN THE WOODS. COLOR A PICTURE OF A DUCK AND ADD IT TO THE PAGE OF THE DAY YOU WENT TO THE POND TO FEED THE DUCKS.   THIS PROJECT IS GOOD FOR 1.) THE EXPERIENCE OF THE ACTIVITY (DAY TRIP- BIRDING, FEEDING THE DUCKS) 2.) ARTS AND CRAFTS PROJECTS THAT CAN BE ADDED TO THE SCRAPBOOK (COLOR, DRAW, PAINTING) 3.) PHOTOGRAPHY 4.) SCRAPBOOKING 5.) JOURNALING

TRY NOT TO TAKE A FULL BREAK. EVEN IF YOU DON'T "OFFICIALLY" SCHOOL DURING THE SUMMER, MAKE SURE THAT THEY DO SOMETHING THAT IS EDUCATIONAL MOST DAYS. YOU CAN DO MATH IN THE POOL WITH MEASURING CUPS AND THE WATER (OR AT THE BEACH WITH THE SAND). EDUCATIONAL EXPERIENCES DON'T HAVE TO BE BORING OR IN A CLASSROOM OR AT THE DINING ROOM TABLE. BE CREATIVE AND HAVE FUN.

DO THE FUN LEARNING ACTIVITIES THAT YOU DID NOT HAVE TIME TO DO DURING THE YEAR. DON'T TELL THE KIDS THEY ARE LEARNING.

TAKE A BREAK PART OF THE TIME, BUT PLAN TO HAVE 2 DAYS A WEEK WHERE YOU CONTINUE HAVING SOME SCHOOL FOR A COUPLE OF HOURS. YOU CAN BE NONTRADITIONAL -- GAMES, MORE SCIENCE EXPERIMENTS, SCRAPBOOKING A TRIP -- BUT DEFINITELY DON'T LET MATH, ALL COPYWORK, PHONICS, AND READING ALOUD GO AWAY FOR THE WHOLE SUMMER.

DON'T LET YOUR BRAIN COMPLETELY CHECK OUT OF SCHOOLING. IT IS TOO HARD TO GET GOING AT THE END OF THE BREAK. KEEP LEARNING BUT JUST DON'T LET THE KIDS KNOW THEY ARE SCHOOLING BY THE THINGS THEY ARE LEARNING (MAYBE THINGS THAT YOU ALL DON'T TYPICALLY DO DURING THE COURSE OF THE SCHOOL YEAR).

DON'T BE TEMPTED TO BE A TEACHER (NOT EVER, BUT ESPECIALLY IN THE SUMMER). JUST RELAX AND WATCH WHAT YOUR KIDS NATURALLY GRAVITATE TO SO YOU CAN KNOW BETTER WHAT TO INVEST IN FOR THEM WHEN FALL ROLLS AROUND AND ALL THOSE MAGICAL HOMESCHOOL CATALOGS COME IN THE MAIL.

SHORTER BREAKS (1-2 WEEKS AT A TIME) THROUGHOUT THE YEAR SEEM TO WORK BEST FOR US IN SUBJECTS LIKE MATH, SO THAT NO ONE GETS RUSTY. WE USUALLY DO ONE BREAK EARLY IN SUMMER, AND ONE BREAK AT THE END. HOWEVER, AS RELAXED-SCHOOLERS, WE DON'T REALLY EVER STOP "DOING SCHOOL". ALL THROUGH THE YEAR WE DO READ-ALOUDS AND INDIVIDUAL READING, VARIOUS WRITING ACTIVITIES, AND LEARNING ABOUT OTHER SUBJECTS THROUGH BOTH OUR READING AND THE VARIOUS ACTIVITIES WE PARTICIPATE IN. FOR US, SUMMER IS JUST A CHANGE OF PACE INSTEAD OF A BREAK FROM LEARNING.

FOCUS ON SPENDING TIME ENJOYING YOUR CHILDREN AND PLAYING WITH THEM. STOP MAKING EVERY MOMENT TEACHABLE AND HOLD DEAR THE MOMENT! PLAY CATCH AND FRISBEE, RIDE BIKES; LOVE THEM WITH YOUR TIME AND ENERGY.

LET THE KIDS FIND THINGS TO DO. THEY WILL DEFINITELY DO SO. DON'T TRY TO OVER SCHEDULE THEIR TIME. THEY NEED TO HAVE THE FREEDOM TO LEARN TO ENTERTAIN THEMSELVES AND LEARN FROM THEIR OWN ADVENTURES. HAVE LOTS OF FUN.

TRY NOT TO CONFORM IT TO THE PUBLIC SCHOOLS' BREAK PERIOD, MAKE ONE THAT WORKS FOR YOUR FAMILY. 'SUMMER BREAKS' DO NOT HAVE TO BE STRICTLY DURING SUMMER, YOU KNOW.

BE CONFIDENT ENOUGH TO CHOOSE WHAT WORKS WELL FOR YOUR FAMILY - WHETHER THAT MEANS TAKING A BREAK BECAUSE MOM NEEDS IT EVEN IF OTHER FAMILIES SCHOOL YEAR ROUND, OR IF IT MEANS WORKING THROUGH THE SUMMER EVEN IF YOUR CHILDREN AREN'T THRILLED TO DO THAT. YOU CAN CHOOSE WHAT WILL BE THE MOST BENEFICIAL TO YOUR FAMILY.

DON'T BE AFRAID TO TAKE A BREAK! SO MANY PEOPLE THINK THEY CAN USE THE SUMMER TO "CATCH UP" WITH THE PUBLIC SCHOOL KIDS...IF THEY ONLY KNEW, THAT MOST PUBLIC SCHOOLS DON'T FINISH THEIR CURRICULUM AND THE PUBLIC SCHOOL KIDS ARE BEHIND THE HOMESCHOOLING KIDS. SO, DON'T WORRY - YOU ARE WHERE YOU ARE SUPPOSE TO BE - PUT YOUR WORRIES AND CARES INTO OUR HEAVENLY FATHER'S HANDS AND LET HIM FILL YOU WITH HIS PEACE.

LOOK AT IT AS A MORE RELAXED VERSION OF WHAT YOU DO DURING THE REST OF THE YEAR. KIDS NEVER STOP LEARNING. THEY LEARN TO ENTERTAIN THEMSELVES, SELF-CONTROL, CREATIVE ARTS, ATHLETICS AND A MYRIAD OF OTHER SUBJECTS EVEN THOUGH THE BOOKS ARE CLOSED. TAKE ADVANTAGE OF THIS GLORIOUS TIME TO ENJOY THEM AND MODEL JESUS FOR THEM.

I THINK THE MOST IMPORTANT THINK IT TO DO SOMETHING, ANYTHING, TO KEEP GOING. AT LEAST HAVE THEM READ SOMETHING EVERYDAY, OR READ TO THEM EVERYDAY.

TAKE THE TIME TO READ UP ON DIFFERENT CURRICULUM, HOW-TO BOOKS, AND GATHER THE MATERIALS YOU NEED. IT IS HELPFUL TO ORGANIZE YOUR SCHOOL BEFORE IT STARTS....THAT WAY YOU DON'T FEEL SO SCATTERED.

I FIND I STILL HAVE TO HAVE SOME TYPE OF LOOSE SCHEDULE TO HELP GIVE US DIRECTION. RELAX AND BUILD FAMILY RELATIONSHIPS AND LASTING MEMORIES. KEEP A ROUTINE EVEN IF IT IS NOT "SCHOOL".

HOME EDUCATION IS NOT "SCHOOL" SO KEEP LEARNING, OBSERVING AND ENJOYING GOD'S CREATION EVERY DAY EVEN DURING "SUMMER BREAK" (JUST DON'T MAKE A BIG DEAL OF IT)!

ENJOY THE OUTDOORS AS MUCH AS POSSIBLE.

FIND SOME FUN THINGS THAT YOUR CHILDREN LIKE TO DO THAT YOU TYPICALLY SAY "WE DON'T HAVE TIME FOR" AND DO THEM. PLAY GAMES. GO ON TRIPS. LEARN A NEW SKILL. HAVE FUN AND UNWIND.

DON'T TAKE TOO MUCH TIME OFF. DO TINY BITS EACH DAY SO THE KIDS DON'T LOSE KNOWLEDGE OR THEIR "SCHOOL SPIRIT".

DON'T BURN YOURSELF OR YOUR FAMILY OUT BY DOING "TOO MUCH". WE PLAN ON HAVING SCHOOL OFF AND ON THROUGHOUT THE SUMMER MONTHS. WE'LL BE TAKING BREAKS HERE AND THERE, BUT WE'LL ALWAYS HAVE DAILY READING TIME AND QUIET TIME.

BE SPECIFIC ABOUT EXPECTATIONS AT THE BEGINNING SO THE KIDS KNOW HOW LONG THE BREAK IS AND WHEN SCHOOL STARTS AGAIN THIS WAY THERE ARE NO SHOCKS OR SURPRISES WHEN SCHOOL COMES AROUND AGAIN. MOST THINGS CAN BE A LEARNING EXPERIENCE. THEY DON'T ALWAYS HAVE TO KNOW THEY ARE LEARNING. HAVE FUN WITH IT.

DON'T FEEL GUILTY ABOUT RELAXING. AND DON'T FORGET TO TAKE TIME TO SKETCH OUT A ROUGH PLAN OF WHAT YOU WANT TO ACCOMPLISH NEXT SCHOOL YEAR.

TAKE TIME TO ENJOY JUST BEING "THE MOM"... AND LET THE KIDS TAKE THE LEAD WITH THEIR DISCOVERIES AND INTERESTS. TAKE TIME TO REFUEL YOURSELF SO THAT YOU WILL BE A BETTER MOM, AND TEACHER, IN THE FALL.

SNAP PHOTOS, KEEP PAMPHLETS, TICKET STUBS, POSTCARDS, PROGRAMS, ETC OF ALL YOU DO AND SEE. YOU'LL BE AMAZED AT HOW MUCH YOU HAVE DONE AND HAVE A RECORD OF IT.

DON'T FORCE LEARNING, BUT DON'T WASTE THIS TIME EITHER. LEARNING CAN HAPPEN ANYTIME, ANYWHERE. LET LIFE TEACH ALL OF YOU. LEARN TOGETHER AND HAVE FUN.

STOP THINKING LIKE PUBLIC SCHOOLS. SCHOOL THROUGH THE SUMMER, WITH BREAKS, SO THAT YOU CAN SCHOOL THROUGH THE WINTER WITH MORE BREAKS.

READ, READ, READ!!!

DEPENDS ON YOUR SITUATION OF COURSE, BUT I WISH I'D HAD SOMEONE HELP ME FORMULATE AND WRITE OUT A/MY BIBLICAL PHILOSOPHY OF EDUCATION BEFORE I STARTED ON OUR HOME EDUCATION JOURNEY ~ IT WOULD HAVE MADE THINGS EASIER IN TERMS OF FINDING THE LORD'S WILL WHEN IT CAME TO OUR JOURNEY. WE DID A LOT OF TRIAL AND ERROR AND WHILE THE LORD REDEEMS EVERYTHING IN OUR LIVES, HAVING DONE THINGS THE HARD WAY, I GLADLY TELL FOLKS NOW THAT IF WE'D ASKED THE LORD TO SHOW US HIS PHILOSOPHY OF EDUCATION TO BEGIN WITH, WE'D HAVE DONE SOME THINGS QUITE DIFFERENTLY. :) CHARACTER TRAINING ~ WHICH IS ALWAYS ON-GOING OF COURSE, BUT IN SUMMER WHEN THERE IS LESS FOCUS ON ACADEMICS, IT'S A GOOD TIME TO MAKE SURE THAT OUR CHARACTER QUALITIES ~ OURS AND OUR CHILDREN'S ~ ARE BEING TRAINED TO GOD'S STANDARDS. BY THE TIME SEPTEMBER COMES AROUND GOOD CHARACTER HABITS HAVE HAD A CHANCE TO BECOME INGRAINED. :)

REALIZE THAT FORMAL LEARNING IS ONLY ONE ASPECT OF EDUCATION. EXPERIENCE, TRAVEL, WORKING JOBS--THERE ARE MANY WAYS TO DEVELOP NECESSARY SKILLS FOR LIFE.

DON'T TAKE A "BREAK". MAKE THE MOST OF YOUR TIME "OFF"!

STILL KEEP A SCHEDULE, BUT CHANGE IT UP A BIT.   KEEP LEARNING, BUT TAKE IT OUTSIDE AND DO LOTS OF FIELD TRIPS AND FOLLOW YOUR CHILD'S LEAD ON WHAT INTERESTS THEM AND FIND A WAY TO BRING IT BACK TO LIFE AT HOME... IF YOU'RE AT THE ZOO, FIND OUT WHAT ANIMALS THEY LIKE AND THEN LEARN ABOUT THOSE ANIMALS... WHERE THEY'RE FROM... WHAT THEY EAT, ETC.

TAKE TIME TO LET YOUR KIDS RELAX AND FEEL THAT THEY ARE "OFF" FOR A BIT. UTILIZE YOUR FREE TIME TO "CATCH UP" AROUND THE HOME OR SOCIALLY/FAMILY AND PREPARE FOR THE NEXT "SEMESTER".

CONTINUE LEARNING AND ENJOYING BEING TOGETHER. LEARNING NEVER STOPS. IF YOU HAVE BEEN WANTING TO REALLY EDUCATE YOUR CHILDREN RATHER THAN JUST DOING "SCHOOL AT HOME", THE SUMMER IS THE PERFECT TIME FOR YOU TO READ AND EXPLORE BOOKS WITH YOUR CHILDREN, AND FILL YOUR DAYS WITH MEANINGFUL DISCUSSIONS AND CONVERSATION. KEEP A RECORD OF ALL THE THINGS YOU TALK ABOUT AND DO EACH WEEK, AND YOU WILL BE AMAZED AT HOW MUCH EVERYONE LEARNS!

ENJOY THE BREAK FROM REGULAR ACADEMICS AND FIND NEW EXTRA "LEARNING" EXPERIENCES. ONES THAT GIVE YOU TIME TOGETHER AS A FAMILY AND YOUR CHILDREN DON'T REALIZE THAT THEY ARE BEING TAUGHT. THEY ONLY KNOW THEIR HAVING FUN.

DON'T LET THE LEARNING STOP! CREATE A MORE RELAXED, BUT FUN ENVIRONMENT FOR LEARNING. CHALLENGE YOUR KIDS TO ASK MORE QUESTIONS WHEN YOU'RE OUT ON FIELD TRIPS OR CAMPING, ETC. HAVE THEM KEEP A NATURE OR SUMMER JOURNAL TO WRITE OR DRAW THE THINGS THEY ARE DISCOVERING WHETHER IN THE BACKYARD OR ON VACATION. YOU'LL BE AMAZED AT HOW WIDE OPEN THEIR EYES WILL BE HUNTING FOR NEW FACTS!

DO THE FUN STUFF, BUT DON'T NEGLECT ENTIRELY THINGS THAT ARE EASILY FORGOTTEN IN THOSE MONTHS….YOU WILL BE HAPPIER WHEN THE 'NEW' SCHOOL YEAR BEGINS! THERE WILL NOT BE A NEED FOR SO MUCH REVIEW AND RE-LEARNING :O) MATH AND READING ARE MOST NECESSARY.

USE BAKING AND COOKING DURING THE SUMMER FOR LESSONS IN MEASUREMENTS/FRACTIONS. OUR DAUGHTER LEARNED MORE ABOUT UNDERSTANDING FRACTIONS IN THE KITCHEN THAT SHE EVER UNDERSTOOD FROM TEXTS AND MANIPULATIVES.

CHOOSE A FEW GREAT BOOKS (THERE ARE RESOURCES SUCH AS THE 1,000 GREAT BOOKS LIST, OR LET THE AUTHOR'S SPEAK TO NAME TWO FOR IDEAS ON CHOICES) AND MAKE A PLAN TO READ EVERY DAY FROM YOUR BOOK. IT DOES NOT MATTER WHEN.......BEFORE BEDTIME IS GREAT, OR A RAINY DAY DEPENDING ON YOUR WORK SCHEDULE. I LIKE TO HAVE A BOOK THAT IS DIFFICULT FOR OUR 10 YO TO READ (SO THAT HE GROWS ACCUSTOMED TO HEARING UNFAMILIAR WORDS AND PHRASES) THAT I READ TO HIM. I ALSO HAVE A BOOK THAT IS JUST AT HIS LEVEL TO READ OUT LOUD TO ME. THIS WAY HE ENJOYS THIS READING TIME THOROUGHLY BECAUSE HE DOES NOT STRUGGLE WITH TOO MANY NEW WORDS. WE SAVE THOSE FOR *READING LESSONS* TIME :).

LEARNING ISN'T JUST A "SCHOOL MONTHS" ACTIVITY. KIDS NEED TO BE SHOWED HOW THEY CAN LEARN FOR THEMSELVES. I BRING MY KIDS TO THE LIBRARY RELIGIOUSLY HOPING THAT THEY TOO WILL GROW TO LOVE BOOKS.

WE SPLIT OUR "SUMMER BREAK" UP THROUGHOUT THE YEAR. DON'T BE AFRAID TO ARRANGE YOUR SCHOOLTIME TO BEST SUITE YOUR NEEDS. IF YOU NEED THE TIME "OFF" DURING THE HOLIDAY SEASON, USE "SUMMER BREAK" TIME THEN.

PICK ONE ACADEMIC SUBJECT TO CONTINUE -- I RECOMMEND MATH BECAUSE IT IS THE SUBJECT THAT IS MOST EASILY FORGOTTEN OVER A BREAK, BUT PICK ONE AND CONTINUE IT JUST TO KEEP THE BRAIN CELLS LUBRICATED IN THAT WAY.

WE PRETTY MUCH HOME EDUCATE ALL YEAR, WE TAKE BREAKS ALL THROUGHOUT THE YEAR. HOWEVER, DURING BREAKS WE TRY TO CONTINUE W/ THE BASICS -3R'S SINCE THEY ARE REALLY THE FOUNDATION OF LEARNING AND SEEM TO BE "LOST" THE EASIEST... ESPECIALLY MATH. WE TRY TO MAKE IT FUN AND WE MAY EXPLORE AN INTEREST DURING OUR BREAKS, LIKE VISITING MORE MUSEUMS OR THE BEACH OR NATIONAL PARKS.

RELAX AND ENJOY YOURSELF. THE MOST IMPORTANT THING YOU CAN TEACH YOUR KIDS AS HOMESCHOOLING PARENTS IS TAUGHT BY OUR DAILY TREATMENT OF EACH OTHER. IF WE LET OUR KIDS EXPLORE AND TRY NEW THINGS WITHOUT TOO MUCH NAGGING, WE WILL BUILD STRONG, CHARACTER-FILLED PEOPLE WHO WILL BE SUCCESSFUL.

DON'T PACK IT SO FULL THAT YOUR EXHAUSTED AT THE END OF AUGUST.

RELAX, REFRESH, RENEW AND REGROUP FOR THE NEXT YEAR! GET TOGETHER WITH OTHER HOMESCHOOLERS THAT ENCOURAGE AND EXHORT YOU TO BE YOUR BEST.

I HAVE FOUND THAT WHEN WE DO TAKE A SUMMER BREAK MY CHILDREN ARE A LITTLE BEHIND IN THE FALL AND THEY USUALLY COMPLAIN ABOUT STARTING BACK UP. I HAVE DECIDED NOT TO TAKE BREAKS IN THE SUMMER, INSTEAD WE DO A VERY LAID BACK HOMESCHOOL. THIS CHANGES EVERYTHING FOR MY CHILDREN! THEY DO NOT COMPLAIN ABOUT GETTING MORE SUBJECTS IN THE FALL, THEY EXPECT IT. THEY ALSO ARE NOT BEHIND AT ALL, INSTEAD THEY ARE WAY AHEAD OF WHERE WE LEFT OFF THE PREVIOUS "YEAR". WE USE TO TAKE BREAKS IN THE SUMMER, BUT NOW THERE IS ALSO NO PRESSURE TO RUSH AND FINISH ANYTHING! SKIPPING SUMMER BREAK HAS ALSO CHANGED HOW ME AND MY HUSBAND VIEW OUR HOMESCHOOL, WE LOOK FOR MORE OPPORTUNITIES TO TEACH, AND MAKE THINGS MORE FUN FOR THE CHILDREN! MY HUSBAND JUST MADE A COMMENT YESTERDAY ABOUT HOW OUR CHILDREN ARE "NERDS", HE TOOK US ALL TO A HISTORICAL PARK AND ALL OUR CHILDREN [AGES 1 1/2 , 3,5,7 AND 12] WERE SCREAMING AND JUMPING UP AND DOWN BECAUSE THEY WERE SO EXCITED!

DON'T FEEL COMPELLED TO FOLLOW THE PUBLIC SCHOOL ROUTINE OF A 2-3 MONTH BREAK. WE TAKE MULTIPLE BREAKS THROUGH THE YEAR AND SAVE OUR OUTDOOR, MESSY, HANDS-ON LESSONS FOR SUMMER. THEN WE SPEND THE ENTIRE SUMMER "PLAYING" AT SCHOOL. IT FEELS LIKE A BREAK FOR THE KIDS, WHILE MAKING THE REST OF THE YEAR A LITTLE LESS HECTIC.

WE DO KEEP A REGULAR DAILY ROUTINE OF MATH REVIEW AND READING, BUT DON'T SPEND HOURS AT A TABLE. WE USE GAMES TO RECALL MULTIPLICATION FACTS EXPLORE LOGIC. WE SPEND TIME EACH NIGHT AS A FAMILY READING ALOUD OR QUIETLY BEFORE BED (NOT HAVING A TV AT OUR SUMMER CABIN HELPS THIS ROUTINE TREMENDOUSLY...IT MAKES ME WANT TO GET RID OF OUR TV AT HOME!!)

KEEP THEIR MINDS BUSY. DO SOME SORT OF MATH AT LEAST 3-5 DAYS A WEEK SO THAT THEIR SKILLS STAY SHARP AND YOU DON'T SPEND THE FIRST WEEKS OF THE NEW SCHOOL YEAR, REVIEWING. TRY A UNIT STUDY WHERE YOU ALL LEARN TOGETHER ABOUT SOMETHING. IT DOESN'T TAKE A LOT OF PLANNING, JUST ASSIGN EVERYONE A TOPIC AND LET THEM GO TO WORK. DO ANYTHING YOU WANTED TO DO DURING THE SCHOOL YEAR, BUT FELT TOO PRESSURED BY THE BASICS AND RECORD KEEPING, TO DO. YOU CAN ALWAYS PUT IT IN THE RECORDS IN THE FALL.

TAKE ENOUGH BREAK TO REALLY FELL RECHARGED--MOM AND KIDS. DON'T TAKE SO MUCH OF A BREAK THAT YOU WIND UP RETEACHING A WHOLE BUNCH OF STUFF IN THE FALL. IF YOU LIVE IN THE SOUTH, CONSIDER TAKING A "SPLIT BREAK" ON BOTH SIDES OF THE SUMMER HEAT AND HAVE SCHOOL IN JULY AND AUGUST WHEN IT IS REALLY TOO HOT AND BUGGY TO HAVE FUN OUTSIDE--ESP. IF YOU DON'T HAVE A POOL.

RELAX AND DON'T THINK OF SCHOOL FOR AT LEAST A MONTH. THEN GIVE YOURSELF THE FOLLOWING MONTH TO THINK, PRAY AND DECIDE WHAT YOU'LL BE DOING NEXT YEAR.

ENJOY EVERY MINUTE OF THE TIME TOGETHER AND KEEP THE SUMMER AS STRESS FREE AS POSSIBLE. ENCOURAGE CHILDREN TO PLAY OUTDOORS AND USE THEIR IMAGINATIONS AS MUCH AS POSSIBLE.

DON'T INSIST ON A LOT OF PAPERWORK. DO TAKE MANY PHOTOS AND MAKE A SUMMER MEMORY/LEARNING BOOK.

USE THE SUNSHINE, THE GARDEN AND YOUR LOCAL SPORTS FACILITIES TO GET OUT AND ABOUT AND YOU WILL SEE POSITIVE RESULTS IN THE CLASSROOM. ALSO IF YOU HAVE PUT IN A GOOD LONG PERIOD OF SCHOOLING MAYBE TAKE A BREAK AND ENJOY SOME DOWN TIME JUST ENJOYING BEING A FAMILY.

IF YOU HAVE SMALL CHILDREN JUST LEARNING TO READ OR DO MATH FACTS, REMEMBER TO REVIEW SOMEHOW (TRY TO KEEP IT FUN LIKE A GAME) OVER THE SUMMER. IT IS SO DISCOURAGING TO REALIZE THAT THEY "LOST IT" ALL OVER THE SUMMER FROM LACK OF PRACTICE. OLDER CHILDREN MAY ALSO NEED PRACTICE WITH MATH FACTS. ALSO, BE SURE TO PARTICIPATE IN OTHER FUN LEARNING ACTIVITIES SUCH AS GARDENING, FIELD TRIPS, SERVICE PROJECTS, SCRIPTURE MEMORIZATION, HOUSE/YARD CLEANING, ETC. THESE TYPES OF ACTIVITIES KEEP THE KIDS IN THE LEARNING MODE WHILE ALLOWING THEM TO HAVE A LITTLE MORE FUN AND BE A LITTLE BIT MORE FREE. ALSO, DON'T FORGET TO GET YOUR BOOKS, LESSON PLANS (OR AT LEAST AN IDEA OF WHAT YOU WILL TEACH AND HOW), SCIENCE EXPERIMENT MATERIALS, AND OTHER SUCH THINGS READY FOR THE NEXT SCHOOL YEAR. THIS GIVES YOU THE CHANCE TO GET FAMILIAR WITH NEXT YEAR'S MATERIALS INSTEAD OF HAVING YOU TRY TO WORK HARD TO STAY A LITTLE AHEAD OF YOUR STUDENTS ALL YEAR!

DON'T STOP ENTIRELY. WE TAKE A BREAK WHILE THE KIDS ATTEND CAMP. WHEN WE COME BACK, WE ARE ON OUR SUMMER SCHEDULE. THE KIDS GO OUT TO PLAY IN THE COOLER MORNING HOURS AND WE DO SCHOOL IN THE AFTERNOON WHEN IT'S TOO HOT TO BE OUTSIDE.

DON'T GET LAZY! TAKE A BREATHER, SLOW DOWN THE PACE AND RELAX, BUT SLOWLY START PLANNING FOR THE FALL. JUST ENJOY TAKING A BREAK, HOWEVER BRIEF. MAKE PLANS TO DO SPECIAL "SUMMER-ONLY" ACTIVITIES THAT YOUR CHILDREN CAN LOOK FORWARD TO EACH YEAR.

TAKE A BREAK!! SOME PARENTS ARE SO FOCUSED ON HAVING "SUPER KIDS" THAT THEY FORGET THAT EVERYONE NEEDS TO RELAX, BREATHE AND ENJOY EACH OTHER. A BREATHER GETS EVERYONE READY TO DIVE IN TO A NEW SCHOOL YEAR WITH ENTHUSIASM. GET HOOKED UP WITH YOUR LOCAL LIBRARY'S READING PROGRAM. THEY HAVE GREAT WAYS TO ENCOURAGE KIDS TO READ, OFTEN WITH LITTLE PRIZES ALONG THE WAY. MY KIDS SPEND 1/2 OF THEIR SUMMER READING BOOKS THEY ENJOY, AND I CAN HEAR THE DIFFERENCE IN THEIR VOCABULARIES BY THE SUMMER'S END. WHEN TRAVELING WITH YOUNGER KIDS, WE GET BOOKS ON TAPE (WELL, CD THESE DAYS) SO THAT THE CHILDREN (AND MOM AND DAD) CAN LISTEN TO GOOD STORIES AS THE MILES PASS BY. SERIOUSLY CONSIDER IF A SUMMER BREAK IS WHAT YOUR FAMILY NEEDS, OR IF THAT IS WHAT YOU ARE USED TO. IT MAY SEEM LIKE A NICE BREAK FOR YOU, BUT IN THE LONG RUN, IT MAY BE MORE TROUBLE THAN IT'S WORTH.

TAKE THE BREAK AND DON'T STRESS! WHEN IT FEELS RIGHT THEN DO SCHOOL. BUT DON'T TRY TO PROVE ANYTHING BY DOING SCHOOL. SOME SUMMER IT MAY CLICK. A BREAK IS BETTER.

DON'T WORRY ABOUT A LITTLE BACKSLIDING. WE'VE SEEN A LITTLE BACKSLIDING IN SOME SUBJECTS, BUT IN OTHERS WE'VE OFTEN SEEN MORE PROGRESS, EVEN THOUGH WE HAVEN'T BEEN MAKING THE CONSCIOUS EFFORT.

REMEMBER THAT LEARNING IS A PART OF EVERY DAY LIFE. EVEN IF YOU AREN'T USING BOOKS DURING THE TIME OFF FROM SCHOOL, TAKE ADVANTAGE OF THE OPPORTUNITIES AROUND YOU TO LEARN AND TEACH.

STAY IN TUNE WITH YOUR CHILDREN, I WOULD NEVER LEAVE OUT DEVOTIONS AND READING ALOUD!

ENJOY THE BREAK!! BE PROUD OF YOUR ACCOMPLISHMENTS FROM THE RECENTLY COMPLETED YEAR OF HOMESCHOOLING. TAKE TIME EACH WEEK DURING SUMMER BREAK TO DO SOME PREP WORK FOR THE NEXT SCHOOL YEAR...IT JUST MAKES IT EASIER TO GET BACK INTO TEACHING FULL-THROTTLE WHEN THE SCHOOL YEAR BEGINS AGAIN. ENJOY IT. BUDGET YOUR TIME WELL BECAUSE IT IS EASY TO LET IT SLIP BY AND WONDER WHERE THE TIME WENT. USE AT LEAST PART OF YOUR BREAK TO PLAN FOR THE UPCOMING SCHOOL YEAR SO WHEN IT COMES YOU CAN START WELL.

MAKE SURE YOUR "BREAK" IS JUST FROM FORMAL SCHOOL WORK AND NOT FROM DISCIPLINE OR FROM GOD...!

EVERY FAMILY IS DIFFERENT--DO WHAT YOU NEED TO DO!

RECOGNIZE THAT IT WILL BE HARD TO START UP AGAIN, SO PLAN TO START JUST A FEW MORNINGS A WEEK, AND BUILD UP YOUR WEEK. DON'T STRESS, HOMESCHOOLING HAPPENS EVEN WHEN YOU DON'T REALIZE IT.

DON'T WORRY ABOUT TRYING TO FORCE OPPORTUNITIES TO STILL LEARN OVER THE SUMMER. SO MANY THINGS HAPPEN NATURALLY THAT THERE WILL BE PLENTY OF OPPORTUNITIES TO TAKE A "LEARNING MOMENT."

PLAY! PLAY! PLAY OUTSIDE AS A FAMILY!! OBSERVE NATURE TOGETHER.

DON'T CALL IT A BREAK. OUR CHILDREN THINK SCHOOL IS PART OF MOST DAYS, AND IT'S EASIEST NOT TO CHANGE THAT TOO MUCH.

LOOK FOR WAYS TO EXTEND ON WHAT YOU'VE BEEN STUDYING OR PREVIEW WHAT YOU WILL STUDY NEXT YEAR IN A "REAL WORLD" CONTEXT. SHOWING KIDS HOW THE THINGS THEY ARE STUDYING APPLY TO LIFE MAKES THEM SEEM MORE RELEVANT AND VALUABLE AND IS ALSO A SNEAKY WAY TO KEEP THINGS FRESH IN THEIR MINDS. :)

STARTING A LOOSE SCHEDULE ABOUT A WEEK BEFORE "SUMMER BREAK" ENDS HELPS EASE THE TRANSITION BACK FOR BOTH MOM AND CHILDREN. IT ALSO GIVES YOU A "HEADS UP" ON WHAT CHARACTER ISSUES MIGHT NEED TO BE ADDRESSED THE COMING SCHOOL YEAR. :-)

FIRST AND FOREMOST I'D SAY GO WITH THE FLOW OF WHAT YOU THINK WILL WORK FOR YOUR FAMILY. IF IT DOESN'T WORK PERFECTLY, YOU'LL NATURALLY MAKE CHANGES HERE AND THERE. IT TOOK OUR FAMILY ABOUT 3 YEARS OF HOMESCHOOLING TO ACTUALLY FIGURE OUT WHAT THAT LOOKED LIKE IN OUR HOUSE. AS FAR AS WHAT HAS WORKED FOR OUR FAMILY, I'D RECOMMEND AT LEAST KEEPING TO 1-3 SUBJECTS THROUGHOUT THE SUMMER. AND FOR THE FREE TIME, YOU MIGHT CONSIDER SCHEDULING IT TO SOME EXTENT. CERTAIN TIMES FOR MEALS, SITTING AND EATING TOGETHER, CERTAIN TIME-FRAMES FOR CHORES, FOR OUTSIDE PLAY, MAYBE QUIET TIME, PRAYERS, ACTUALLY MAKE THE DAYS RUN MORE SMOOTHLY AND NOT GET HECTIC AND ROWDY. ALSO, LOOK INTO WHAT YOUR COMMUNITY OFFERS. MANY LIBRARY DISTRICTS OFFER MORE TO FAMILIES DURING THE DAYS IN THE SUMMER. FREE SUMMER CONCERTS ARE COMMON. AND EVEN FREE DAYS AT MUSEUMS, ZOOS OR OTHER PLACES OF INTEREST. PLAN SEVERAL OUTINGS, MAYBE ONCE A WEEK TO KEEP THE FUN FEELING OF SUMMER BREAK AND HAVE A LITTLE TWIST TO YOUR NORMAL SCHOOLING ROUTINE. LASTLY, DON'T TRY TO DO EVERYTHING YOU FIND OUT ABOUT! IT SEEMS THE LONGER WE SCHOOL THE MORE AND MORE WE FIND OUT IS AVAILABLE TO US. ALMOST EVERYTHING SOUNDS JUST WONDERFUL AND EXCITINGLY EDUCATIONAL FOR THE KIDS. THE KIDS WILL GET A MARVELOUSLY FINE EDUCATION WITHOUT DOING EVERYTHING AVAILABLE TO THEM. IN FACT, THEY MAY HAVE A BETTER EDUCATION WITH A LITTLE TIME TO BREATH THE FRESH AIR AND SIMPLY THINK AND PLAY.

WHEN OUR CHILDREN WERE YOUNG AND ACTIVE, I LIKED TO HAVE THE HOLIDAYS PLANNED OUT WITH AN EXCURSION OR ACTIVITY FOR EACH DAY. NOW THAT THEY ARE OLDER WE ALL ENJOY THE BREAK AND A TIME TO RELAX AND DO SOME OF THE THINGS WE JUST DON'T USUALLY GET THE TIME FOR... I GUESS ITS GOOD TO DEVELOP TRADITIONS.. WE HAVE CERTAIN THINGS THAT WE ALWAYS DO DURING THE SUMMER BREAK.
THERE ARE ALWAYS LOTS OF COMMUNITY EVENTS GOING ON SO IT'S WORTH CHECKING WITH THE LIBRARY. CAN BE LOTS OF FUN TO HAVE SOME THEME DAYS. AGAIN, WHEN THEY WERE YOUNGER, I USED TO STOCK UP ON CRAFT BOOKS AND CRAFT MATERIALS, AND ALWAYS HAD SOME IDEA UP MY SLEEVE.

THEY THINK THEY'RE TAKING A BREAK BECAUSE THEY ARE DOING SOMETHING FUN. I LET MY KIDS KNOW LEARNING IS FUN BY THE FUN THINGS THEY DO AND STILL LEARN WHILE HAVING FUN.

PICK A DATE AND STOP EVEN IF BOOKS AND WORKBOOKS AREN'T FINISHED. STOP FOR AT LEAST TWO WEEKS TO RECHARGE.

RELAX AND ENJOY, REALLY SOAK UP LOTS OF NON-HOMESCHOOL TIME FILLED WITH LEARNING AND YOU'LL FIND YOUR CHILDREN WILL 'LEARN' SO MUCH MORE THAN YOU EVER EXPECTED.

MAKE A PLAN OF LITTLE BY LITTLE DE-CLUTTERING THE SCHOOL MATERIALS AND LABEL THINGS YOU PUT AWAY. THROW AWAY WHAT YOU DON'T NEED, GIVE AWAY THOSE GOOD MATERIALS THAT JUST DON'T FIT IN YOUR HOMESCHOOLING BUT OTHERS CAN BENEFIT FROM THEM. AND REST (THIS ONE IS GOOD AT ALL TIMES THOUGH :)

HERE'S THE TRUTH. OUR FIRST YEAR OF HOMESCHOOLING I SET THE YEAR UP JUST LIKE THE PUBLIC SCHOOL TIME SET. THE NEXT YEAR, I WAS ABLE TO BREAK AWAY FROM MY EXTREMELY TRADITIONAL MINDSET AND SET THE YEAR UP TO BETTER FIT OUR FAMILY AND CLIMATE. SO WE ACTUALLY START OUR SCHOOL YEAR THE FIRST WEEK OF JULY (IT'S TOO HOT

OUTSIDE TO DO MUCH ANYWAY EXCEPT MAYBE GO SWIMMING). THIS LEAVES US WITH SOME TIME TO ENJOY THE MORE COMFORTABLE WEATHER OUTSIDE IN THE FALL EITHER TO HAVE A SCHOOL BREAK OR GO ON FIELD TRIPS. WE TRY TO FINISH OUR SCHOOL WORK BY MAY SO WE CAN ENJOY A LITTLE SPRINGTIME OUTSIDE. SO OUR SUMMER BREAK IS BASICALLY MAY AND JUNE, GIVE OR TAKE A FEW DAYS.

PRAY AND ASK FOR WISDOM WHAT TYPE OF BREAK IS BEST FOR YOUR FAMILY, THIS YEAR.

Our summer schedule:

Summer Day Trip Ideas:

Possible Vacation Ideas:

Things we need to keep
working on through the
summer:

Books that would be great for
Summer reading:

Books we have read so far:

My own favorite books from
my childhood that I want my
kids to know:

Other Summer activities we can participate in:

HOMESCHOOL AND THE HOLIDAYS:

DON'T START DECORATING FOR CHRISTMAS UNTIL AFTER THANKSGIVING IS OVER. OTHERWISE, THANKSGIVING WILL BE "DROWNED" IN THE CHRISTMAS PREPARATIONS, AND WON'T HAVE MUCH MEANING FOR YOUR YOUNG ONES.

DO WHAT IS IMPORTANT TO YOU AND YOUR FAMILY. DON'T STRESS YOURSELF IF YOU CAN'T DO IT ALL. I DON'T THINK MARTHA STEWART HOMESCHOOLS! JUST ENJOY WHAT YOU CAN WITH YOUR FAMILY, EVEN IF IT'S JUST ONE THING.

START OFF SIMPLE, SHARE MEMORIES AND TRADITIONS FROM YOUR CHILDHOOD. ASK THE "GRANDS" WHAT THEY DID IN THEIR DAY. YOU WILL HEAR MANY PRECIOUS STORIES!

I THINK IT IS IMPORTANT, REGARDLESS OF YOUR BELIEF SYSTEM, TO HAVE RITUAL AND ROUTINE IN THE YEAR. KIDS LOVE IT AND IT GIVES THEM A SENSE OF THE PASSING OF TIME. THE MORE RITUALS YOU CAN INCORPORATE INTO YOUR FAMILY ROUTINE EACH YEAR, THE BETTER. BUT ONLY TRY ADDING A COUPLE AT A TIME. SEE HOW THEY FIT YOUR FAMILY AND THEN NEXT YEAR ADD IN A LITTLE MORE. FIND SPECIAL FOOD, SONGS, ACTIVITIES, STORIES, EVEN CLOTHES YOUR FAMILY WOULD ENJOY AND DO IT YEAR AFTER YEAR; BECAUSE THOSE YEARS FLY BY QUICKLY AND YOUR CHILDREN WILL REMEMBER THOSE TRADITIONS ALWAYS.

A WHOLE UNIT STUDY COULD BE MADE USING THE SUBJECT OF COLONIAL AMERICA. YOU WOULD BE TEACHING HISTORY. YOU COULD FIND SOME OF THE MUSIC OF THE TIME AND LEARN ABOUT THAT FOR MUSIC. A SAMPLER COULD BE MADE FOR LIFE SKILLS. MATH SKILLS WOULD BE USED BY BUILDING SOMETHING OF THE ERA. PE COULD BE DONE BY PLAYING GAMES OF THE TIME. IF THE CHILD COULD MAKE UP A STORY OF A FICTIONAL FAMILY OF THE TIME, THEY WOULD BE USING LANGUAGE ARTS.

TEACH MATH THROUGH BAKING AND MEASURING. REMEMBER THAT LEARNING CLEANING SKILLS IS A LIFE SKILL AND NEEDS TO BE TAUGHT AS WELL AS ACADEMIC SKILLS.

TAKE TIME TO ENJOY THE SEASON TOGETHER. DON'T BE COMPULSIVE ABOUT FINISHING ACADEMIC SUBJECTS TO THE POINT THAT YOU IGNORE THE OPPORTUNITIES FOR MAKING MEMORIES. TEACHING OUR CHILDREN TO BE GIVING TO OTHERS AT THIS SEASON IS OF MAJOR IMPORTANCE. EVEN IF THEY DON'T HAVE MONEY TO BUY GIFTS, THEY CAN MAKE GIFTS, OR GIVE OF THEIR TIME. TEACH CHILDREN TO REALLY LISTEN TO OTHERS, ESPECIALLY LONELY ELDERLY FOLKS. THEY CAN ALSO DO YARD WORK OR HOUSEWORK TO HELP THESE FOLKS.

ALSO, START MAKING PLACEMATS, NAPKIN RINGS ETC., EARLY SO YOU WON'T BE IN A RUSH WHEN THANKSGIVING COMES AROUND. THE CHILDREN WON'T BE TIRED EITHER AND IT WILL BE A JOYOUS OCCASION WHEN IT IS TIME TO DECORATE, NOT A BURDEN.

FOR MEMORIZATION HAVE EACH CHILD TAKE A VERSE IN TURN. WORK ON THEM EVERY DAY AND BY THE TIME EACH CHILD HEARS THEIR SIBLING REPEAT THEIR VERSES THEY SEEM TO AUTOMATICALLY LEARN THE OTHER CHILDREN'S AS WELL! IT ALSO HELPS TO ACT THEM OUT AT LEAST WITH HAND MOTIONS.

THINK ABOUT WHAT YOU MIGHT DO NOW. IF YOU WAIT UNTIL DECEMBER, YOU'LL NEVER DO IT. ALSO, DON'T PLAN SO MANY THINGS THAT YOU DON'T FINISH ANY OF THEM.

WE USE AN ADVENT CALENDAR FROM WHICH WE PULL OUT SOME FUN, QUICK ACTIVITIES IDEAS THAT DON'T REQUIRE A LOT OF WORK, BUT REMINDS US OF THE SEASON. PERHAPS ONE SAYS, "SING A CHRISTMAS CAROL--ALL VERSES!" WE MAY READ A STORY, WRAP A GIFT, MAKE A PHONE CALL, OR DECORATE THE FRONT DOOR. WE SPEND AN HOUR OR SO ON A SATURDAY COMING UP WITH IDEAS TO PUT INSIDE OUR CALENDAR.

MAKE YOUR PREPARATIONS PART OF YOUR SCHOOL DAY INSTEAD OF IN ADDITION TO YOUR REGULAR SCHOOL DAY.

I WOULD SAY TO PLACE THE FORMAL BOOKS AND SCHEDULE THAT YOU HAVE BEEN USING COMPLETELY ASIDE. PLEASE DON'T WORRY ABOUT FEELING LIKE YOU ARE "FALLING BEHIND" OR "OFF SCHEDULE." THE SPIRIT OF THE SEASON IS ABOUT LOVE. THIS MEANS SPENDING TIME WITH YOUR FAMILY. THIS MEANS YOU MUST BE EXTRA CAREFUL AT THIS TIME OF YEAR NOT TO OVER-SCHEDULE YOURSELF WITH OUTSIDE ACTIVITIES. WHY NOT JUST TAKE AN AFTERNOON AND SPEND IT WITH GRANDMOTHER (OR OTHER FAMILY MEMBERS) OVER COFFEE, HOT CHOCOLATE, AND COOKIES? EVERYONE WOULD ENJOY THAT MORE THAN ANYTHING ELSE. WHY? BECAUSE YOU ARE GIVING EACH OTHER THE GIFT OF TIME. THIS IS THE GREATEST GIVE THAT WE CAN GIVE EACH OTHER IN THIS WORLD. I KNOW THAT THIS IS MUCH EASIER SAID THAN DONE. SO, I WOULD SAY TO STOP, SLOW DOWN, AND THINK SERIOUSLY ABOUT THE TIME YOU SPEND AND HOW YOU SPEND IT, ESPECIALLY DURING THIS BUSY HOLIDAY SEASON. REMEMBER, PEOPLE ARE MORE IMPORTANT THAN ANYTHING. THE PEOPLE IN OUR LIVES ARE GOD'S GIFTS TO US, AND WE SHOULD TREAT THEM AS SUCH. AND, DON'T FORGET TO KEEP GOD IN YOUR ACTIVITIES...

DON'T HOMESCHOOL VERY LONG INTO DECEMBER. TAKE THE ENTIRE THANKSGIVING WEEK OFF.

USE FAMILY TRADITIONS AND STORIES, OR MAKE UP YOUR OWN NEW ONES. INVOLVE THE WHOLE FAMILY. MAKE IT FUN. ASK YOUR CHILDREN WHAT THEY WOULD LIKE TO DO.

THE KIDS ALWAYS HELP WITH THE FOOD PREP FOR THANKSGIVING AND CHRISTMAS, MAKING GOODIE BASKETS FOR NEIGHBORS AND MAKING OUR CHRISTMAS CARDS TO SEND TO FRIENDS AND FAMILY. IT'S A GOOD WAY TO INCORPORATE DOING THINGS FOR OTHERS WHILE WORKING ON MEASURING SKILLS, ART SKILLS AND HAND EYE COORDINATION.

1. START SMALL!

2. CHOOSE ONE OR TWO THINGS THAT CAN BECOME A "FAMILY TRADITION."

3. READ INSPIRING "HOLIDAY" STORIES ALOUD TO THE FAMILY. (MY KIDS LOOK FORWARD TO THE EXTRA STORY ON FRIDAY NIGHTS.)

4. CHOOSE A "FAMILY SONG" TO SING THAT IS ASSOCIATED WITH THAT "HOLIDAY."

MAKE NOTEBOOK PAGES ON THE HISTORY OF, OR ALL ABOUT A HOLIDAY. FIND GREAT BOOKS TO READ ALOUD ON THE HOLIDAY.

A LOT OF TRADITIONAL FAMILY ACTIVITIES CAN BE GEARED TOWARD HOMESCHOOLING WITH A LITTLE ADDED EMPHASIS ON THE LEARNING ASPECT OF EACH TRADITION AND ACTIVITY.

MAKE THEM FUN AND AGE APPROPRIATE. A FOURTH GRADER DOESN'T WANT TO MAKE A DANCING TURKEY ANYMORE AND A FIRST GRADER DOESN'T WANT TO FIND THE TRUE MEANING OF CHRISTMAS.

TAKE TIME TO SHARE GOD'S LOVE WITH THOSE AROUND YOU BY DOING WHAT GOD ENABLES YOU TO GIVE EVEN IF IT IS YOUR TIME TO A SHUT IN OR AN ELDERLY NEIGHBOR OR BABYSITTING FOR A YOUNG MOTHER. THIS HAS BEEN THE BEST WAY FOR OUR CHILDREN TO LEARN TO GIVE OF THEMSELVES AND TO GIVE EVEN WHEN WE DON'T HAVE MUCH. MAKE THE WHOLE HOLIDAY PREPARATIONS YOUR HOME EDUCATION FOR THE MONTH OF DECEMBER AT LEAST.

MAKING CHRISTMAS CARDS IS LANGUAGE ARTS/WRITING. BAKING IS MATH AND SCIENCE. READING GREAT READ-ALOUDS FOCUSED ON THE HOLIDAY. MEMORIZING SCRIPTURE PERTAINING TO THE HOLIDAY. MAKING GIFTS AS ART. CAROLING-MUSIC CARD MAKING-ART BUYING GIFTS-MATH BAKING-HOMEEC/MATH CHRISTMAS IN OTHER COUNTRIES-GEOGRAPHY GIVING TO THOSE LESS FORTUNATE-COMMUNITY SERVICE YOU DON'T HAVE TO TAKE DAYS OFF OVER THE HOLIDAY SEASON IN ORDER TO GET IT ALL DONE. YOU JUST HAVE TO INCORPORATE IT INTO YOUR "SCHOOL" DAY! MAKE IT FUN AND THEY'LL NEVER KNOW THEY ARE LEARNING AND THINK THEY ARE NOT EVEN DOING SCHOOL.

THE BIGGEST TIP I HAVE IS ONE I WAS GIVEN BY A FELLOW HOMESCHOOLER, AND THAT IS TO TAKE THE ENTIRE MONTH OF DECEMBER OFF OF REGULAR HOMESCHOOLING SO YOU CAN CONCENTRATE ON THE FUN FAMILY ACTIVITIES OF THE HOLIDAYS WITHOUT GETTING OVERWHELMED BY ALL OF THE CHOICES. EVEN IF IT MEANS EXTENDING YOUR REGULAR SCHOOL YEAR A LITTLE, I THINK YOU AND YOUR CHILDREN WILL FIND IT WELL WORTH IT. CHRISTMAS SHOULD BE A RELAXING TIME OF FAMILY CELEBRATION OF THE GREATEST GIFT EVER!

WORK AHEAD OF TIME SO THAT YOU CAN TAKE THE ENTIRE MONTH OF DECEMBER OFF. NOTHING SAYS 'SCROOGE' LIKE A GROUCHY HOMESCHOOL FAMILY FLYING THROUGH THE HOLIDAYS IN A FRANTIC HURRY!

IT'S IMPORTANT TO FOSTER THE FEELINGS OF THANKSGIVING YEAR-ROUND -- NOT JUST IN NOVEMBER. SAME WITH CHRISTMAS. IF WE FOCUS ON CHRIST'S BIRTH ONLY IN DECEMBER, THEN IS IT ANY WONDER THAT OUR CHILDREN GROW UP TO SEGMENT THEIR CHRISTIANITY INSTEAD OF LIVING IT AS A WHOLE.

RELAX ABOUT SANTA CLAUS. AT LEAST WHERE I LIVE, PARENTS GET REALLY WIGGED OUT OVER THIS. I EXPLAIN TO THEM THAT THERE IS NO CIRCUMSTANCE WHERE A WELL-MEANING ADULT TELLING A CHILD THAT THERE IS NO SANTA EVER SUCCESSFULLY DID THAT CHILD A FAVOR. I THEN ENCOURAGE THEM IN OUR FAITH - THAT, WHEN PRACTICED, OUR RELIGION IS SO RICH THAT SANTA CAN'T HELP BUT FADE INTO THE BACKGROUND.

HOMEMADE GIFTS ARE THE HIGH SPOTS OF OUR HOMESCHOOL LESSONS. WE LEARN ABOUT ALL KINDS OF THINGS DEPENDING ON WHAT TYPE OF PROJECT WE DECIDE UPON. FOR EXAMPLE, WE ARE GOING TO BE MAKING NATIVITY SCENES WITH POLYMER CLAY THIS YEAR. WE WILL LEARN CHEMISTRY BY STUDYING HOW THE CLAY IS MADE AND THE CHANGES IT GOES THROUGH TO HARDEN. MATH IS USED TO DETERMINE HOW MUCH OF EACH COLOR CLAY IS NEEDED, AND HOW MUCH MONEY WILL BE SPENT ON EACH PROJECT. HISTORY AND ART WHEN WE DISCUSS THE ARTISTIC STYLE THAT WE USED TO CREATE THE NATIVITY, ETC.

EITHER FIND WAYS TO INCORPORATE IT INTO WHAT YOU ARE DOING - (FRACTIONS = BAKING) OR TAKE A SHORT BREAK FROM SOME OTHER LESSONS TO DO THE HOLIDAY STUFF INSTEAD. I DON'T LIKE TO ADD IT ON TOP OF EVERYTHING ELSE - TOO MUCH STRESS AT THIS TIME OF YEAR. TRY TO MAKE LESS WORK FOR YOURSELF, NOT MORE. FOR EXAMPLE - INSTEAD OF YOUR REGULAR ART LESSON, LET YOUR CHILDREN MAKE HOMEMADE WRAPPING PAPER. IF THEY ARE OLD ENOUGH TO HANDLE SCISSORS, LET THEM WRAP FOR YOU. GRANDMA AND GRANDPA (AND YOUR CHILD) WILL LONG REMEMBER A HOMEMADE WRAPPED GIFT THAT WAS NOT WRAPPED LIKE YOU WOULD DO IT OVER ONE THAT LOOKS LIKE A PICTURE. LET THE LITTLE THINGS GO AND ENJOY YOUR CHILDREN IN THIS BLESSED SEASON. AND - THIS IS THE ONE TIME I FOLLOW THE LEAD OF THE PUBLIC SCHOOL AND TAKE A BREAK. WE WILL BE "OFF SCHOOL" FROM A FEW DAYS BEFORE CHRISTMAS TO A COUPLE OF DAYS AFTER NEW YEARS.

JUST ABOUT ANY HANDS-ON PROJECT THAT TIES A HISTORIC EVENT TO A HOLIDAY WILL BE REMEMBERED. ESPECIALLY IF THE PROJECT CAN BE SHARED WITH ONE OR MORE OTHER FAMILIES

IT WOULD BE A GOOD SOCIAL STUDIES UNIT TO STUDY OTHER COUNTRIES BY STARTING WITH THE HOLIDAYS AND HOW THEY CELEBRATE THEM, TRYING OUT DIFFERENT FOODS, ETC. (ALSO A GREAT WAY TO "CONVERT" A PICKY EATER!)

MAKE A MUMMY AND DADDY TAPE/CD CONTAINING A HOST OF MATERIAL RELEVANT AND HELPFUL FOR EACH CHILD NARRATED BY PARENTS AND PERSONALIZED FOR EACH CHILD. CAN INCLUDE SCRIPTURES FOR MEMORY WORK, EXHORTATIONS, SONGS, STORIES, LOVE AND PRAISE NOTES, TEACHINGS (PARTICULARLY ON CHARACTER ISSUES), AND EDUCATIONAL CONTENT. VARIETY OF MATERIAL AND VOCAL QUALITY OF MOM AND DAD (ENTHUSIASM, SINCERITY, LOVING, GENTLE...) ARE TWO KEY POINTS FOR SUCCESS. CHILDREN WILL TREASURE IT.

MAKE A BLESSING TREE, FOR THANKSGIVING. WE DRAW A TREE ON POSTER BOARD AND EVERYDAY WE PUT LEAVES ON IT, THAT WE HAVE WRITTEN WHAT WE THANKFUL FOR.

DON'T TRY TO DO A 'REGULAR' SCHEDULE & DUMP HOLIDAY STUDIES ON TOP OF IT. YOU WILL STRESS OUT YOURSELF, YOUR KIDS, AND YOUR SPOUSE! (AFTER ALL, THEY HAVE TO LISTEN TO YOU TRYING TO FIGURE OUT WHY THIS ISN'T WORKING!)   RELAX & TRY A MORE 'UNIT STUDY' APPROACH. WE AREN'T 'UNIT STUDY PEOPLE' BUT FROM NOVEMBER 1ST THROUGH EPIPHANY, THIS WORKS THE BEST --- WE'RE STILL READING, WE'RE STILL STUDYING HISTORY, WE'RE STILL GETTING SOME MATH & SCIENCE & GRAMMAR ~ BUT ~ WE'RE MUCH MORE RELAXED ABOUT IT & MORE ABLE TO FOCUS ON THE SEASON!

IT IS A TIME OF GIVING TO OTHERS (GETTING INVOLVED WITH AN ORGANIZATION THAT HELPS THE NEEDY), WITNESSING ABOUT THE LOVE OF JESUS (CAROLING AT A NURSING HOME), INVITING A FAMILY OVER (MAYBE A FAMILY WHO DOESN'T HAVE CLOSE FAMILY AROUND THEM) TO DECORATE GINGERBREAD HOUSES OR HOLIDAY COOKIES.

PLAN EARLY OR THE TIME FLIES BY.

WHEN TEACHING SPECIAL NEEDS, AS I IMAGINE IS THE CASE WITH 'NEUROTYPICAL" STUDENTS, LOOK FOR AND YOU WILL FIND TEACHABLE MOMENTS. SOCIAL STUDIES/COMMUNITY SKILLS: VOLUNTEERING IS IMPORT AS IT TAKES THE FOCUS OFF OF SELF AND DIRECTS ENERGY IN THE MINISTRY OF HELPING OTHERS. FUNCTIONAL ACADEMICS (MATH & SCIENCE) AND SELF-CARE SKILLS ARE LEARNED AND REINFORCED IN THE KITCHEN. SHOPPING, MEASUREMENT, WRITING, REASONING SKILLS, ETC ARE ALL NECESSARY TO INDEPENDENCE. HISTORY: USING HANDS ON (WE USE UNIT STUDIES - IN THE HANDS OF A CHILD) WE ALL LEARN FROM HISTORY. IT GIVES THE SPECIAL LEARNER A SENSE OF BELONGING, TO FAMILY, COMMUNITY, NATION. IT IS IMPORTANT GOD'S TRUTH BE A REALITY IN THE HEART - THAT WE ARE EACH UNIQUELY CREATED AND IMPORTANT - AND GOD GIVEN EACH AND EVERY ONE OF US A MINISTRY.

KEEP A NOTEBOOK FOR IDEAS THAT OCCUR TO YOU THROUGHOUT THE YEAR. MAKE A FEW PAGES FOR EACH HOLIDAY AND JOT DOWN IDEAS AS YOU RUN ACROSS THEM ON THE NET OR THINK OF THEM. THIS CAN INCLUDE ANYTHING, FROM CRAFT IDEAS, TO BAKING, TO DECORATING, AND MORE. YOU'LL BE AMAZED AT THE NUMBER OF IDEAS YOU COME UP WITH, AND HAVING THEM ALL IN A NOTEBOOK MEANS YOU DON'T HAVE TO SIT AND TRY TO COME UP WITH SOMETHING THE DAY BEFORE A HOLIDAY. WHAT ARE SOME OF THE TRADITIONS YOU REMEMBER AS A CHILD? WHAT DO YOU WANT TO PASS ALONG TO YOUR CHILDREN, AND WHY? WRITE THEM DOWN AND PLAN TO INCLUDE THEM.

WE ESPECIALLY LIKE CELEBRATING THE ADVENT SEASON, COMPLETE WITH CANDLES, HYMNS AND BIBLE READINGS; KEEPS US FOCUSED THROUGHOUT THE WHOLE OF DECEMBER.

HOLIDAY UNIT STUDIES ARE A GREAT WAY TO INCORPORATE THE HOLIDAYS INTO SCHOOL. JEWISH HOLIDAY STUDIES ARE VERY INTERESTING, THE LIFE CYCLE OF AN EVERGREEN TREE CAN BE STUDIED, ASTRONOMY CAN BE TIED IN, CULTURAL STUDIES (HOW OTHER CULTURES CELEBRATE), ETC.

RELAX AND ENJOY THE SEASON. MAKE WORSHIPING OUR SAVIOR THE #1 PRIORITY THROUGHOUT THE SEASON. ACADEMICS CAN BE INCORPORATED INTO ALL THE ASPECTS OF PREPARING FOR THE CELEBRATION OF GOD'S LOVE FOR US. RATHER THAN THINKING OF LOST "SCHOOL" TIME DURING THE HOLIDAYS, THINK OF SPECIALIZED EDUCATION AS YOU HAVE THE OPPORTUNITY TO TEACH MEANINGFUL ETERNITY-LESSONS AND TIMELESS MEMORIES.

IT'S THE SIMPLE THINGS LIKE READING THE CHRISTMAS STORY TOGETHER OR MAKING ORNAMENTS OR DECORATING THE HOUSE WITH PAPER SNOWFLAKES THAT THE CHILDREN MADE, THAT REALLY MEAN THE MOST. IT GIVES YOU AN OPPORTUNITY TO TEACH WITHOUT "TEACHING".

I'D SAY JUST START SMALL--ONE FAVORITE BOOK OR ACTIVITY, AND ENJOY THAT TO THE FULLEST. THEN ADD SOMETHING ELSE IF TIME ALLOWS. WE TEND TO FEEL WE HAVE TO GO ALL OUT ON EVERYTHING WE DO, AND OFTEN DON'T START IMPORTANT THINGS IF WE CAN'T SPEND A WHOLE BUNCH OF TIME ON IT.

ALSO, DON'T FORGET ABOUT AN ELDERLY OR DISABLED NEIGHBOR OR FRIEND - EVEN A STRUGGLING SINGLE PARENT. YOU'D BE SURPRISED HOW A LITTLE REMEMBRANCE BRINGS SUCH JOY. CAN YOU SHOVEL THEIR WALK, MOW THEIR YARD, TRIM THEIR BUSHES, TAKE OUT THEIR TRASH, FIX AN APPLIANCE - GIVE OF YOURSELF? GIVING OF YOURSELF MEANS SO MUCH MORE, AND WE ALL NEED TO REMEMBER THIS.

FINISH ALL YOUR WORKBOOK TYPE LESSONS IN THE MORNING SO YOU CAN HAVE THE AFTERNOON TO WORK ON HOLIDAY CRAFTS AND CURL UP ON THE COUCH WITH ALL THE KIDS TO READ "A CHRISTMAS CAROL" OR WORK ON HOLIDAY HANDICRAFTS WHILE LISTENING TO CINNAMON BEAR OR OTHER HOLIDAY RADIO THEATER/BOOKS ON CD (SEE HOMESCHOOLRADIOSHOWS.COM FOR A GREAT HOLIDAY STORIES COLLECTION!).

I WOULD KEEP MY EYE ON THE NEWSPAPERS AND SMALL MUSEUM WEBSITES. I FIND THAT THE SMALLER MUSEUMS MAY HOLD OFF ON ACTIVITIES UNTIL THE HOLIDAYS BUT THEY MAY HAVE ACTORS AS AUTHORS, STORYTELLERS, ETC. I LIKE TO HOLD OFF ON REALLY HEAVY DUTY HOLIDAY STUFF UNTIL CLOSE TO THE HOLIDAYS SO THE KIDS DON'T GET BURNED OUT BY THE TIME MID DEC ROLLS AROUND. PLUS HERE IN THE NORTHEAST, JAN AND FEB ARE COLDER (AND SOMETIMES MORE BORING) THAN DECEMBER SO HAVING A FEW IDEAS "LEFTOVER" FROM THE HOLIDAYS GIVES US A GOOD PICK-ME-UP WHEN THE DOLDRUMS HIT.

I THINK THAT WE HAVE A WONDERFUL OPPORTUNITY TO BLEND SCHOOL WITH HISTORY AND THE HOLIDAYS. I START WITH FALL AND WE TALK ABOUT THE ABUNDANT BLESSINGS WE HAVE IN HARVEST. WE LOOK FOR THE NEEDY AND GIVE TO BLESS THEM. WE DO POETRY AND TALK ABOUT THE CHANGES IN THE SEASON. DURING THANKSGIVING WE REMEMBER ALL THAT TOOK PLACE FOR US TO HAVE OUR FREEDOMS. WE TAKE TIME TO REALIZE THAT GOD HAD HIS HAND IN EVERYTHING. IT SURE HELPS US BE EVEN MORE THANKFUL. THE DAY AFTER THANKSGIVING WE START READING THE CHRISTMAS STORY FROM THE BIBLE. WE ALSO BEGIN USING THE CHRISTMAS STORY FOR OUR COPYWORK. IT'S REALLY AMAZING TO SEE ALL THE REALLY GREAT CONVERSATIONS THAT EVOLVE FROM THIS ACTIVITY. MY CHILDREN ACTUALLY LOOK FORWARD TO IT EVERY YEAR. WE ALSO USE THE JESSE TREE WHICH IS A TYPE OF ADVENT. IT'S FULL OF SCRIPTURE. THERE ARE SO MANY THINGS TO DO. BASICALLY IT'S JUST TAKING THE TIME TO PLAN AND MAKE SOME REALLY GOOD MEMORIES PUTTING TREMENDOUS FOUNDATIONS IN YOUR CHILDREN'S LIVES.

PICK ONE MAJOR ACTIVITY (HISTORY POCKET, LAP BOOK, CELEBRATING ADVENT, WHATEVER) AND DO ONLY THAT - DON'T GO CRAZY TRYING TO DO IT ALL.

PRAY ABOUT IT FIRST. ASK GOD TO POINT TO THOSE ADDITIONS OR REPLACEMENTS THAT WOULD BE MOST BENEFICIAL IN DEVELOPING YOUR FAMILY'S FAITH AND GROWING RELATIONSHIP WITH HIM. ASK FOR HIS INSIGHT INTO WHETHER A CHANGE IN ROUTINE WOULD BE HELPFUL OR HARMFUL FOR YOUR CHILDREN AT THIS POINT AND ASK THIS FREQUENTLY THROUGH THE YEAR. THEN, START WHERE ALL ARE COMFORTABLE. MAYBE YOU SIMPLY ADD SOME SINGING TO YOUR DAY. THIS MAY END UP BEING A NEW HABIT FOR THE YEAR!! OR TAKE THE OPPORTUNITY TO TEACH HOSPITALITY WITH AN OPEN HOUSE OR BY GATHERING THOSE WHO HAVE NO FAMILY NEAR TO CELEBRATE WITH YOURS. TEACH SOME HOME EC WITH CHRISTMAS TREATS OR MATH BY FIGURING HOW LONG TO COOK THE TURKEY. TAKE WALKS AS A FAMILY TO EXPERIENCE THE CHANGING WEATHER AND TALK ABOUT HOW WE ARE BLESSED BY THE SEASONS OR HOW WE SEE GOD'S CONSTANCY IN THE SEASONS. OR JUST SET ASIDE YOUR ENTIRE NORMAL ROUTINE TO DIG INTO HOW GOD MOVED IN HUMAN HISTORY TO ADVANCE HIS PURPOSES AND WE END UP WITH HOLIDAYS AND STORIES AND SONGS TO CELEBRATE THIS. ENJOY!

WHEN MY KIDS WERE YOUNG, TOO MANY CHRISTMAS-Y ACTIVITIES MEANT THAT THEY GOT OVER EXCITED AND COULDN'T LEARN. I FOUND THAT A BALANCE IS NEEDED!

WE START OUR SCHOOL YEAR IN JANUARY, AND WE SCHOOL YEAR ROUND. WE GOT OUR 180 DAYS COMPLETED IN LATE SEPTEMBER, SO EVERYTHING WE DO FOR THE REST OF THIS YEAR IS FOR FUN. THE WEEK OF THANKSGIVING, WE PUT THE BOOKS AWAY AND PLAN FUN ACTIVITIES FOR THE REST OF THE YEAR. THIS YEAR, WE'RE PLANNING LOTS OF COOKIES AND CANDIES FOR PRESENT PLATTERS, AS WELL AS A GINGERBREAD HOUSE AND SERVING IN OUR CHURCH'S LIVING NATIVITY.

I THINK LOOKING AT THE HISTORY OF HOLIDAYS AND THEIR CELEBRATION IS GREAT. ALSO, TRYING TO BETTER UNDERSTAND THE TRUE SIGNIFICANCE OF HOLIDAYS IS ALSO GREAT. USING READINGS AND JUST DISCUSSION HAS BEEN OUR BEST WAY OF UNDERSTANDING HOLIDAYS.

FAMILY READINGS IN THE EVENINGS. TAKE TURNS READING ALOUD. CHRISTMAS SNACKS, CUDDLED UP IN A SPECIAL PLACE - A WONDERFUL FAMILY (EDUCATIONAL!!) ACTIVITY!!

KISS -- KEEP IT SIMPLE SWEETIE!!   REMEMBER WHOSE BIRTHDAY IS BEING CELEBRATED (JESUS' BIRTHDAY--NOT YOURS OR THAT OF ALL THOSE AROUND YOU) AND CELEBRATE HIM, NOT OURSELVES IN OUR GIFT GIVING.

Our 'Holiday Season' homeschool schedule:

Our family's traditional
holiday activities:

Things we could do to make our holidays better:

Ways we can incorporate the holidays into our homeschooling:

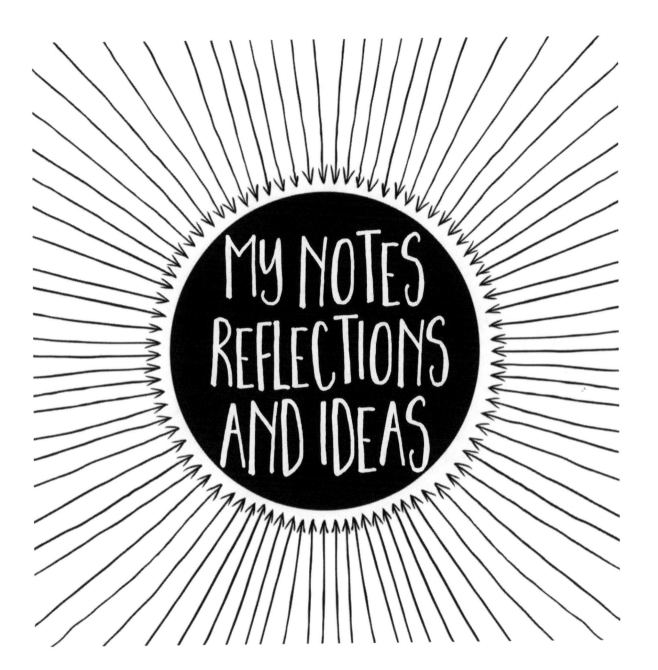

If I could make one change in our homeschooling, it would be...

What is working GREAT in our Homeschool:

What areas need improving in our homeschool:

Character Qualities we need to work on:

My goals for our homeschool this year

Favorite Ideas from this Journal:

Notes to myself:

Notes to Myself:

Made in the USA
Middletown, DE
07 March 2016